H.R.F. Keating

MEERA TAMAYA

H.R.F. Keating: Post-Colonial Detection

A Critical Study

Bowling Green State University Popular Press
Bowling Green, OH 43403

For Giri

Acknowledgements

First and foremost, my special thanks to Bette Loholdt, English/Communications Department Secretary, whose intelligence, computer wizardry and patience with the fractious English faculty is legendary. Bette has made sense of my illegible scrawls, garbled interviews on tape, and borne with bracing wit my gripes and vacillations. Thanks also to the Chief Librarian for Public Services and Collection Development, at North Adams State College, Suzanne Kemper, for her incredible resourcefulness in answering my sometimes unanswerable reference questions. Louise Ouelette, Library Assistant for Inter Library Loans, actually told me that she liked receiving requests for interlibrary loans, thereby absolving me of guilt for making constant demands on her. Thanks. My walks and talks with Marilyn Kurata, a fellow detective fiction addict, gave me the idea for this book. Finally, I must thank the subject of this study, H.R.F. Keating, for patiently answering all my questions, and his wife, Sheila Mitchell, for her hospitality.

Contents

Introduction

Detective fiction, that Cinderella of literary forms, has grown so accustomed to her glass slippers that she not only dances all night with such suitors from academia as Umberto Eco and Roland Barthes, but globetrots as far as China and India. Long a stepchild of literature, either neglected or abused by critics, detective fiction is now the subject of learned debates. One critic goes so far as to claim that it provides the kind of deep structure to contemporary post-modern literature that psychology and myth did to modernism (Holquist 165). Since its heyday in the 1920s, detective fiction has grown so much in number and kind, that we can no longer divide detective fiction into just two major categories: the golden age British and the American hardboiled mysteries. Van Gulik's China novels and James McClure's South African novels have taken the genre to other realms and more expansive concerns. Similarly H.R.F. Keating, the subject of this book, who started out as a quintessentially British writer in the tradition of Conan Doyle and Agatha Christie, found his true calling writing about the multifaceted Indian subcontinent, as he chronicles the misadventures of Inspector Ghote of the Bombay police.

How would one categorize the work of H.R.F. Keating, who has written a total of 39 novels,

1

assorted radio plays, and books on detective fiction, but whose claim to fame rests on the 17 award-winning Ghote novels? Perhaps we can find a clue in the reasons he chose to write mysteries. In his autobiographical notes and interviews Keating talks about how he had nursed a secret desire to become a writer for years without actually doing anything to fulfill his dreams because he felt he had nothing to say. When his wife learned of his ambition, she pointed out that he could write detective novels because "they don't say anything." With her encouragement he wrote 11 very British, very orthodox mysteries in the tradition of Agatha Christie. However, the novels enjoyed only a modest success because, as one publisher informed him, they were too British. Ironically, it was only after he abandoned the tidy British form and went on to write the Ghote novels that he found fame and acclaim. The setting of the Ghote novels are not only a far cry from the cozy English village, but the characters also bear no resemblance to the familiar British stereotypes popularized by the Golden Age novelists. Finally, and perhaps most important, far from not having anything to say, Keating ends up saying a good deal about deeply felt moral issues. Every one of Ghote's investigations involves a moral dilemma. Talking about the choice Ghote makes in his latest book *The Iciest Sin*, Keating says, "I asked myself what I would do in a terrible dilemma. I know I wouldn't necessarily do the right thing" (Interview 1).

This statement has several implications. First, Keating's explorations of ethical concerns place the novels closer to the tradition of Nineteenth Century English moralists. Indeed, in his most recent interview, Keating admits that, "One of my editors was always ribbing me about being a moralist. I think you are perfectly right that I am in the Forster tradition." His mention of E.M. Forster is particularly apposite because Forster's best known novel, *A Passage to India*, explores moral issues against the vexing issue of British imperialism and racism. Keating's modus operandi is similar. In every mystery that Ghote investigates, Ghote, every inch an Indian in cultural trappings, serves as a mouthpiece for Keating's own consciousness.

This "doubleness" of Ghote—an Indian functioning as a British author's alter ego—has consequences for Keating's experimentation in the form of the detective novel as well as his innovations in the character of the detective. It also raises the question of how Indian Ghote really is and what place the novels occupy in the broad spectrum of British writing in India.

It is my contention that because Ghote, although recognizably Indian, is really a mask, in the Yeatsian sense, for Keating, the novels are deeply subjective in a way that traditional mystery novels are not. As Michael Holquist argues, it is not a coincidence that the popularity of the mystery genre soared at the time when modernist realistic fiction, influenced by depth psychology and studies in myth, plumbed the darkest regions of the psyche in the hands of such practitioners as Thomas Mann, James Joyce and D.H. Lawrence. According to Holquist, the puzzle form of the mystery ensured that the author did not take off into the stratosphere of philosophical inquiry or plunge into the fathomless depths of the psyche, and thus provided the reader with an escape not so much from life as from literature. In support of this argument he points out that the most ardent fans of detective fiction are literate academic types. By contrast, Keating's novels straddle, however precariously, the mystery-as-puzzle genre as well as the realistic novel with its emphasis on subjectivity. Indeed, at one point Keating set himself the challenge of putting in as little murder as possible in a murder story. In his very first award winning novel, *The Perfect Murder*, for example, the victim recovers from a blow to his head by that old standby, the blunt instrument.

What holds the reader's interest in the Ghote novels is the way every vibration of Ghote's psyche is recorded. This is true of all the Ghote novels as Ghote simultaneously investigates a mystery as well as a moral-philosophical conundrum. The charge leveled against the mystery genre by such academic heavyweights as Edmund Wilson, that characters in the genre are mere stereotypes, does not apply to Ghote who emerges as one of the most introspective, deeply human characters in detective fiction. It is Ghote's minutely observed consciousness which makes the novels closer to modern, realistic fiction while retaining the investigative interest of mystery fiction.

Besides adding depth to the sterile puzzle form, the figure of Ghote rings a unique variation on the character of the supersleuth. From Holmes onward, most detectives in the British genre have been aristocratic amateurs who investigate for the cerebral pleasures of puzzle solving. Lord Peter Wimsey and Albert Campion are the blue-blooded ancestors of even such a modern professional as P.D. James'

Adam Dalgliesh. They are not your average flatfooted British Bobby who, if they appear on the scene at all, serve as sidekicks to better set off the brilliance of a Wimsey or a Campion. Besides being superbrains, the aristocratic amateur sleuths are supremely self assured and at home in the world of so called "high" culture—Holmes plays a Stradivarius and Wimsey collects rare manuscripts and opera singers. They are also cocooned in the glamour of their class and possess all the heroic virtues—courage and integrity—while their flaws are merely endearing eccentricities. They look on their world with a sense of irony, a privilege of the aristocrat who is above the vulgar scramble for mere survival.

Inspector Ghote of the Bombay police is the very antithesis of all this. He is a hopelessly bedeviled professional, hamstrung by the mysterious ways of Indian bureaucracy, bullied by his boss and nagged by his wife. Far from being brilliant, Ghote solves crimes more by dogged persistence and flashes of intuition than by superior ratiocination. Also, unlike Holmes with his aquiline nose and his pipe, Poirot with his pointed waxed moustaches, Ghote has no distinguishing physical features. He remains a physically shadowy figure. The author occasionally refers to his thin bony shoulders. We are given no other details. It is hard to visualize him and he is treated by his colleagues and superior as a mere cog in the creaky machinery of the Bombay police force.

What makes this nondescript fellow lovable is that no one is more aware of his own shortcomings than Ghote himself. The author tirelessly records every twitch of his nerves as his multitudinous insecurities threaten to overwhelm him at every turn.

6 H.R.F. Keating

His chronic and nearly crippling feelings of insecurity spring from two factors both of which he is heir to. One is his lower middle-class social status, that perilous perch on the brink of poverty from which, thanks to his education, he can contemplate quality without the wherewithal to buy it. An example of this is a poignantly funny scene in *Inspector Ghote Hunts the Peacock* in which, on arrival at Heathrow Airport, Ghote is humiliated at having to own up to his "cardboardy—no very cardboardy suitcase" even as he is greeted by a representative of Scotland Yard. Also, unlike British sleuths who lead a bachelor existence unencumbered by wife and children, Ghote is burdened by family responsibilities.

The other, more ingrained cause of his feelings of inadequacy, is the legacy of more than a hundred years of British imperialism. His situation is representative of most middle-class Indians who manage to combine in one schizophrenic psyche both Indian and British cultural values. Ghote is Hindu by birth and upbringing, but a member of the Bombay police force, which like the educational, legal and parliamentary systems are inherited from, and modeled on, British institutions. The most obvious example of this curious colonial mutation is Ghote's use of the English language. Like most middle-class Indians, Ghote's English is both fluent and comically inept, and no one is more aware of his mis-pronunciations and grammatical infelicities than he is. He constantly agonizes over whether he is "correct" in his speech or not, especially when he deals with his superiors and British and American visitors. While all this adds to the existential comedy of his situation, it also makes him a deeply sympathetic figure. For after all, how many of us can identify with the godlike eminence of a Holmes or the *outre* arrogance of a Poirot?

Ghote's colonial psyche brings us to the larger question of Keating's portrayal of India. Where does he stand in the vast body of British writing on India? In order to evaluate his contribution to colonial and post colonial writing, one must begin with the genesis of his Ghote series. When asked in an interview about how and why he hit upon India as the locale for his fiction, Keating has said that a major factor in his decision was his perception that his novels did not do well in America because they were too British and "if you are not sold in America you cannot possibly make a living out of writing crime stories." Casting about for an exotic locale that would make his mysteries more marketable, he says he thought of India because "India was *in* that year." Amplifying on this remark he goes on to say, "that India, certainly in the British press, was held up as being a fine example of neutrality. People thought, can there be a way out of the cold war and India a line between?" (Interview 1).

Keating is talking about the early 1960s; his first India novel, *The Perfect Murder*, was published in 1964. Before considering how India's special features suited Keating's needs as a writer, we must examine England's cultural and historical situation which made India particularly attractive to its citizens. The 1960s were a time of cultural upheaval. On the level of popular culture, the Beatles put working-class talents and panache on the map. In the realm of "high" culture, French theorists were aiming their missiles at the ivory towers of academia. As they deconstructed the canon as well as Ian Fleming, the rigid lines between high and low brow literature were obliterated. On the political front, Britain found itself relegated to the status of a minor power in the cold war between the super powers America and the Soviet Union. The nationalization of the Suez Canal in 1956 by Egypt's President Nasser marked the decisive end of England's long reign as the world's foremost imperial power. Even as England suffered the final spasms of its imperial *delirium tremens*, it was seized by a feverish nostalgia for all the exotica associated with its colonies. The Beatles levitated towards India seeking spiritual sustenance and ended up creating a market for Nehru jackets. The influx of immigrants from the disintegrating empire also changed the provincial face of English cities. London's Holmesian fog was dispersing in the winds of spicy ethnic cooking. Living as he does in Notting Hill Gate, it was inevitable that Keating should capture the *zeitgeist*, create Inspector Ghote, and set him on his peregrinations through the varied landscape of India.

Keating's Ghote novels belong in the mystery genre, but they also have to be considered in the broader perspective of British writing on India. From Kipling to Paul Scott, India has provided raw material for the British imagination even as it supplied the natural resources—cotton is just one example—to its ever hungry factories with the finished product, English chintz, sold back to India at extortionate prices. When Queen Victoria declared herself Empress of India the brightest jewel on her crown was literally the diamond, the Kohinoor, from India. Incidentally, Paul Scott's novel chronicling the death throes of the empire bore the eponymous title, *The*

Jewel in the Crown, thus encapsulating the literal and metaphoric wealth that the British derived and continue to derive from India.

In his monumental study of British and French representations of the orient titled, *Orientalism*, Edward Said points out that "When Disraeli said in his novel *Tancred* that the East was a career, he meant that to be interested in the East was something bright young Westerners would find to be a consuming passion; he should not be interpreted as saying that the East was only a career for Westerners" [3]. For Keating however, interest in India started out as a profitable career move, but it soon became a passion, not so much for the country as for *knowledge* of it.

In Foucaultian terms, acquisition of knowledge is a precondition for control. In Keating's case, with the passing of empire, it is one way of retaining imaginative if not political control. Having set his novels in an exotic locale he had never visited, he must have been driven to compensate for his lack of firsthand experience by learning about India from every possible source. He has talked about his exhaustive research and tireless observation of Indian immigrants in London. He studied, among other things, Indian telephone books and railway guides to get a feel for Indian names as well as places.

Indeed, when I first discovered the Ghote novels in the early seventies, soon after my arrival in the United States, I was drawn to them mainly because of their felt authenticity of detail. Here was an author who did not talk about a generic Indian, as many do, but understood the immense cultural and linguistic gulf that exists between Indians from different states and different castes. The differences are invariably manifested in the details of dress, manners, speech and nomenclature. Keating gets these details right, thus avoiding the mistake many seasoned India observers like Ruth Prawar Jhabvallah make, of writing about India as if it were a homogenized whole, as if there is such a thing as an Indian psyche, a subject of much ethnocentric generalization by the West.

Visitors to India often see selected parts of India, mostly erstwhile princely states in the north and the major cities—Delhi, Bombay and Calcutta—and blithely proceed to make assumptions about the whole. What many writers fail to take into account is that India is a loose federation of states, divided along linguistic lines, each with a distinct culture. Added to these often irreconcilable regional differences are the nearly rigid lines drawn according to the intricate caste system which functions like the class system in the West. Thus talking about the typical Indian character is rather like trying to describe a typical European without taking into account the enormous differences, for example, between the French and the Germans. Keating is perhaps the only Western writer I know whose Indian characters are sharply individualized according to their place of origin and their caste.

The most immediately obvious regional and caste differences are to be found in the many varieties of English spoken in India. From the very start of Britain's global colonial enterprise, one major instrument of colonization has been the imposition of English on its subjugated peoples. When Thomas Babington Macauley proposed an English education for Indians, he recognized that the consolidation of the empire necessitated that the bureaucracy, the army, the police etc., needed to learn just enough English to obey and carry out the dictates of the British government. An authoritative and imaginative use of the language was not part of the bargain. Indians were expected to know enough English to serve as bureaucrats who could oil the engines of quotidian life. This they did while at the same time stamping their newly acquired English with the imprint of a distinctively native syntax, diction and accent. The latter varies according to the region and the social class of the speaker. Thus an Indian with advanced degrees, especially in the Humanities, from the prestigious cosmopolitan universities of Delhi, Calcutta, Bombay and Madras tend to speak fluent, idiomatic English while those who receive a technical education from provincial universities bear the strongest influence of their native tongues.

Keating, studying India assiduously from a safe distance, seems to have a more accurate grasp of these intricacies than those who, confronted with India over a brief but intense span of time, are so overwhelmed by the impact India makes on them, that they fail to notice the myriad distinctions. In other words, Keating's imaginative grasp of India did him better service than the actual experience of living in the country did to many western writers. This phenomenon is not unlike Shakespeare's imaginative understanding of an Egyptian Queen. He did not have to be a woman or an Egyptian to present a complex, vivid, believable portrait of Cleopatra. I am not making the absurd claim that Keating's gifts are on a par with Shakespeare's but only underscoring what the poet Keats understood so well: imagination is the dream of truth.

12 H.R.F. Keating

Keating's decision to set his novels in India liberated him in two important ways. First, it freed him from the orderly constraints of the traditional puzzle form of the mystery novel. In a country as vast, as multifaceted as India with its cumbersome bureaucracy, police procedures, although based on the British model, do not proceed with the orderly efficiency of Scotland Yard, or at least its facsimile in fiction. In *A Perfect Murder*, much of the comedy springs from the way many Indians refuse to abide by the strict requirements of police procedures. Invoking police regulations modelled on those of Scotland Yard rarely produce the expected results in a country which has perfected its subversions of alien authority for more than a hundred years. Ghote is foiled at every turn by the cavalier attitudes of his suspects. Nothing proceeds according to plan in a country where planning itself takes second place to improvisation. The loosely structured form of *A Perfect Murder*, unlike the tightly plotted Christie mysteries, for instance, has an improvisatory rhythm. Indeed Keating has said that his idea for the novel originated in his preoccupation with perfectionism:

> Should you do things perfectly or settle for second best?.... I am a perfectionist in aspiration but in achievement I am a second best. I am born with a conscience: determined always to do the right thing. So perfection comes from that. So this was one of the possible themes that was in my mind. I am sorry to say that I thought of India as being marvellously imperfect, which in many ways it is. (*Autobiography Series* 49)

It is interesting and entirely in keeping with the tradition of Western writers—Conrad is a prime example—that Keating should choose to make India the metaphoric vehicle for the projection of his own perceived imperfections. When he tried to satirize his British society in the pre-Ghote mysteries, the results were altogether too conventional, too constrained to be successful. The choice of India as a metaphor for imperfection set him free to spoof the genre as well as question in a radical way British values and social mores. Thus to choose one example (I will discuss the other novels in the ensuing chapters), in *A Perfect Murder*, he succeeds brilliantly in standing the murder mystery on its head by making the botched-murder victim recover at the end. He also demonstrates the humanness inherent in imperfection when he questions the desirability of perfection—a cherished western value. As Keating himself has pointed out, this use of the mystery genre for the exploration of moral and philosophical concerns is not new; it was pioneered by Dorothy Sayers. In *Gaudy Night* there is no murder and the novel is clearly a vehicle for feminist issues. Keating however, takes the spoofing of the traditional form to new and constantly surprising lengths.

A departure from British shores also provided Keating with the distance which brings a certain cold-eyed objectivity to matters cherished back home. Such homespun Western values as order, efficiency, perfectionism, reason, heroism etc. get a drubbing from the Indian penchant for laid-back paradoxes and its attendant relativisms. Judeo-Christian absolutes are washed away by the heavy and invigorating rain of Hindu philosophical conundrums.

As pointed out earlier, Ghote himself overturns all cherished notions of what constitutes a great detective. If Ghote were placed in a British context, he would be at best a wholly comic character, at worst a pathetic one. But in the Indian context he is simply very human. It also allows a British writer to project unacknowledged traits of his own culture on to the Other in time honored fashion. That is, Ghote's bumbling, his inadequacies, his insecurities are not uniquely Indian. Any deeply class-ridden society like England's produces a substrata of individuals who do not conform to the images of the upper class portrayed in literature and who, if they are portrayed at all, do not occupy center stage: they provide comic relief and foils to the uppercrust. By making his detective an Indian, Keating was able to foreground what in England was either ignored or sidelined by upper-class concerns and values.

Finally, what will probably ensure Keating a place in literary posterity is the difficulty of categorizing him. Ostensibly a mystery writer, recognized and rewarded as one because of the brilliant stroke of inventing an Indian detective and letting him loose in that subcontinent investigating criminal and philosophical problems as he bumbles along, Keating has created a unique subgenre which can be fully evaluated only after he has written his last book, which will, happily, not be for another couple of decades.

What follows in this book is an attempt to map Keating's output as it stands at the time of this writing, taking into account his forays into straight fiction, his British mysteries as well as his contribution to the West's ever present preoccupation with reconstructing the Orient. I begin with a biographical essay and the longest section of the book, the second chapter, is devoted to the Ghote novels, analyzing them simultaneously, but in chronological order, their different but related aspects as whodunits, philosophical explorations and post-colonial fiction. The third chapter deals with his justifiably little known traditional mysteries, the fourth provides a brief synopsis of his "straight" fiction and the book concludes with two interviews conducted ten years apart at his home in London.

Genealogy

In his lengthy contribution to *Contemporary Authors Autobiography Series* (Vol. 8), H.R.F. Keating traces his biological and literary ancestry with disarming modesty and understated irony. He creates a picture of himself as a very ordinary, decent human being without any of those neurotic excesses that have marked post-Freudian portraits of writers and authors. He comes across as the very antithesis of the angst-ridden egomaniacal artist figures mythologised in popular biographies or pathographies, as Joyce Carol Oates terms those works which concentrate on the seamier side of famous figures (3).

Keating's solid, middle-of-the-road life derives naturally from his ancestry—he belongs to that strata of British bourgeoisie which has supplied rich material for comedies of manners from Jane Austen to Barbara Pym. Blessed neither with excessive wealth nor bedeviled by poverty, families such as Keating's usually have a general or a vicar or two perched in the family tree, live in comfortable, unpretentious houses and religiously observe the ritual of tea in the garden under the cherry tree. Descended from Anglo-Irish stock going back to Norman invaders, Keating's family boasts a grandfather who was Canon John Fitz Stephen Keating, Chancellor of Saint Mary's Cathedral, Edinburgh, author of the *Agape* and the *Eucharist* in the Early Church, a grandmother's sister,

17

Kathleen Bruce, pupil of Rodin and later wife of Scott, the Antarctic explorer (164). On his mother's side, his grandfather W.H. Clews was the author of two historical romances.

In other words, Keating's immediate forbears were aspiring men of letters—that peculiarly English breed of gentlemen who regard writing not so much as a vocation, but as an avocation, to be pursued not with mad, visionary self-destructive passion, but with dogged determination and steady prolificity. They were, to use Madonna-inspired slang, wannabe Trollopes and Conan Doyles who saw no conflict in pursuing their professions as well as their writing. They also epitomize that quintessentially English concept of a gentleman. As Keating describes it, his ancestors "left me with an ineradicable belief in that mysterious concept of the 'gentleman,' one with duties in life which if acted on, deserve respect" (164).

Keating's father, although a Cambridge man himself, having a "generous streak of the naive in his make up," espoused a "theory about the tremendous usefulness of the University of Life" (166) and feeling the burden of school fees, took his son out of Merchant Taylor's at the age of sixteen and sent him to work as a wartime youth in training in the engineering department of the BBC. When Keating was not operating the studio controls at night, he was busy writing a comic epic which he did not finish. The father had also prudently enrolled his son in a correspondence course at London University before he was conscripted into the army, coincidentally on the very day that the war with Japan ended. It was a wise move because it entitled Keating for a government grant at a university of his choice.

However, Cambridge University, his father's alma mater, rejected him and he applied to Trinity College at Dublin where he was accepted. Trinity turned out to be ideal because, as Keating puts it: "Trinity at that time was a good place for one of my innate modesty. No high-flying intellectual whiz kids were there to greatly overshadow me" (167). Keating flourished in this relaxed atmosphere, and his four years there were spent earning not only a First Class Honours degree, but he also published poems in the college magazine, wrote short stories, began another novel, *The Deep Despair of Oliver Mudd*, took part in stage productions, and founded a literary magazine. Most important, as an accredited member of the literary set found, "Time above all to talk. Talk is the great Irish virtue and vice. I blossomed swinging from talk's benign branches" (167).

After graduating from Trinity, Keating resolved that a writing career was not for him because, "I had, I judged, nothing to say." With the characteristic modesty which may be "one of my major virtues or besetting sin" he opted for a career as a "sub editor, or a composer of headlines, a chopper-down of other people's copy," rising eventually to become a "copy taster," a selector of minor items in such great newspapers as the *Daily Telegraph*, *The Times* and the *Sunday Telegraph* (167). Although he did not write anything during this period of his life, he read voraciously any book termed "great," and took to heart Joseph Conrad's dictum that a writer should "squeeze out of yourself every sensation, every image—mercilessly, without remorse" (167).

Keating's resolve not to try his hand at fiction lasted for eight years, but fate in the form of his wife put his life back on track. In 1953 he was sent by his newspaper to Swinden, Wiltshire, to review a play called *Breach of Marriage* and he promptly fell in love with one of the actresses. A whirlwind courtship was followed by marriage. His wife, the former Sheila Mitchell, was to prove a "powerful" influence who would have no truck with Keating's image of himself as a gentle failure. She resusicated his moribund childhood ambition to be a writer. As mentioned earlier, it was she who was instrumental in his choosing the mystery genre for his first efforts at writing.

His first novel, set in a repertory theatre, though never published, did provide a plot (a *deus ex machina* crashes down on the victim, in the car in which he was to descend) for a novel, *Death of a Fat God*, which he published later. His second novel was rejected, but undeterred, he went on to write his third which was published by Gollancz, publishers of such established luminaries as Dorothy Sayers, Julian Symons and Michael Innes. *Death and the Visiting Firemen* is set against the background of a coach and four trip he had taken in 1953, from Bath to London, to convey loyal greetings on the occasion of the coronation of Queen Elizabeth.

The publication of the novel inspired Keating to break away from the strict conventions of the orthodox whodunit genre. Margery Allingham was a significant influence on him in his efforts to expand the scope of the murder mystery. Keating had occasion to interview Allingham, and during the interview she quoted G.R.M. Hearne, the author of the Sexton Blake novels: "They never mind you putting all you've got into this sort of stuff. They never pay you any more for it, but they don't stop you" (169). Another author whose example also influenced Keating strongly was Graham Greene. Keating admired Greene for his "relentlessness in going for the truth in writing as he says in *Ways of Escape*, 'truthfully enough for the truth to be plain' " (169) and went so far as to copy from *A Burnt Out Case*, much reread: "A writer doesn't write for his readers does he? Yet, he has to take elementary precautions all the same to keep them comfortable." Besides Graham Greene, Simenon's "search for the truth of people" was a formative influence on Keating (170). With his first published novel in hand, inspired by Allingham, Greene and Simenon, Keating determined to use the detective form to say all that he wanted to say. A childhood memory of his father, an idolized figure, telling a lie about a minor traffic violation supplied the theme for Keating's next novel. The theme of lying and lies, which had obsessed Keating for years, found its way into *Zen There Was Murder*.

With this modestly successful beginning and a small advance from the publishers, Keating felt confident enough to quit his job as a *Times* sub editor and produce a novel a year. After three more: *A Rush on the Ultimate* (1961), *The Dog It Was That Died* (1962) and *Death of a Fat God* (1963) Keating made a momentous decision. He decided to set his new novel in exotic India. That large subcontinent seemed a perfect setting for a theme he had in mind: the undesirability of perfection. Like many British writers from Kipling to Paul Scot, Keating, casting about for a vehicle to explore the theme of perfectionism, found it easier to portray the imperfections of another country rather than his own. For scores of Western writers, India, like Egypt and Africa, has served as the metaphoric Other to examine the shadows of their own psyches.

Keating was particularly delighted when, reading up on India, he found that the Parsee community in India had Perfect as a surname. Thus was born the eponymous title, *The Perfect Murder* of his most successful novel to date. It won the Gold Dagger of the Crime Writers Association in America and a Special Edgar award in America and also achieved the dream of success every popular novelist aspires to—it was made into a movie by the well known Merchant-Ivory team. It also launched the bumbling odyssey of the Indian detective Ghote on whose creation alone Keating's claim to distinction rests.

It is astonishing to read that Keating had no thought of writing a series of Ghote novels, for a series certainly followed: one Ghote novel after another, with metronomic regularity, interspersed by three Christie-like whodunits set in England and two "straight" novels. The eight Ghote novels which rolled off the press between 1966 and 1974—Inspector Ghote's *Good Crusade, Caught in Meshes, Hunts the Peacock, Plays the Joker, Breaks an Egg, Goes by Train, Trusts the Heart, Bats Fly Up*, all written before he ever set foot in India—are some of his best. The cardinal factor in this burst of creativity seems to have been Keating's realization that by creating Ghote, he was finally able to put a great deal of himself in his books.

In other words, the ingrained reticence and bourgeois embarrassment at self-revelation ceased to inhibit him because he had found the perfect disguise in the person of an exotic Other, Ghote, an Indian at furthest remove from an Englishman. The traits that would be considered gauche and déclasse in an English gentleman are perfectly acceptable in an Indian to even the most residual post-colonial imagination. In Keating's own words: "Yes, looking back now, I see that, with the simple luck which the novelist V.S. Naipaul once said was what a writer needed most, I had found myself a hero through whom and in whom I could express my every thought, or most of them, and who is someone also, perhaps by virtue of springing from my innermost self, who is a recognizable, three dimensional, multifaceted human being" (172).

When Keating visited India ten years after he first started writing about it (he did so twice, in rapid succession, invited by Air India and later by the BBC followed by two more visits to make the movie version of *A Perfect Murder*), he did so with trepidation. Yet his imaginative grasp of India was so real and so accurate that the usual things which discombobulate foreigners—the beggars, the lepers, the heat—did not faze him. And yet the details of Indian life made such an impact on him that when he started a short story, he found he was filling pages with observed minutiae, and he could not get to the story. He observes, echoing the poet Keats' paean to the imagination: "I saw the error of my new way, and I hope afterwards did not allow myself to be dragged down by sticky facts from the real world instead of being buoyed up by airy ones passed through the transfiguration factory of the imagination" (174).

In Keating's first post-India novel, *Filmi, Filmi, Ghote* does not benefit from this Keatsian insight into the transfiguring nature of imagination. The novel, set in India's version of Hollywood, termed Bollywood, satirizes the film-industry. An all too easy target, all the characters are cardboard figures and the plot creaks along yoked to the tinseltown's own unintentionally parodic recreation of *Macbeth*. The next novel, set outside Bombay is far more successful, as Keating returns to his metier, the exploration of a moral conundrum—how does liberalism sour into conservatism—as he portrays a retired judge who contemptuously disregards a threat to his life.

His next India novel, the *Murder of a Maharajah* which has only a tenuous connection to Ghote (his grandfather, a schoolmaster solves the crime) is a delightful spoof of the hedonistic lives of princes while it is at the same time a semi-serious exploration of *homo ludens*. The Maharajah of the title is addicted to playing games, but of a deadly sort. Keating returns to Ghote in *Go West Inspector Ghote* and the *Sheriff of Bombay*. The former takes Ghote to L.A. to investigate a religious cult and the latter explores the twin themes of sexuality and subjectivity.

At the time of this writing Ghote shows every sign of slipping into moral quagmires from which he cannot retrieve himself. *Under the Monsoon Cloud* and *The Iciest Sin* have Ghote committing increasingly unbelievable infractions of the legal code. In *Cloud* he helps his superior dispose of a body, thus becoming an accessory after the fact, and in *Sin* after watching a man commit a murder and letting him go free, Ghote is nearly driven to commit a murder himself. "What Next for Inspector Ghote," the reader feels compelled to ask.

Although Keating is justly famous as the author of mysteries, especially the Ghote novels, he has also written "straight" novels, "period" novels set in the Edwardian era published under the pseudonym Evelyn Hervey, assorted short stories featuring the cockney charwoman Mrs. Craggs as sleuth, and nonfiction books on the history and aspects of crime fiction. He has also written radio plays, some featuring Inspector Ghote, and edited five substantive books on crime writers from Agatha Christie to G.K. Chesterton. All this while regularly turning out reviews of detective fiction for the *London Times*. For a man who initially decided not to pursue a career as a writer because he had nothing to say, he has said plenty.

At the time of this writing, he is 65, with a solid body of published work behind, and I suspect, before him. Unlike say, Hemingway, who put a gun to his head fearing that his writing days were over, Keating who has not revealed any of the manic elation/depression cycles of many writers, will probably continue to produce a book a year, and however uneven their overall merit, will have to be reckoned with as one of those prolific authors, like Trollope and his hero Graham Greene, for instance, whose vast presence in the library is hard to ignore. It is hard to predict in what direction he will go, since his persistent moral concerns make him bend the limits of the mystery genre in unexpected directions. As mentioned earlier, Ghote has almost ceased to be a policeman in moral and procedural matters, and it is hard to foresee his future. But Keating has consistently surprised himself and his readers, and with his reputation already well established, he is secure enough to continue to surprise and delight.

In his autobiographical essay for the *Contemporary Authors Series* (Vol. 8) he asks himself rather wistfully whether if he had written about Ghote "more warmly (though from my distance I do not think I fail to see him in a warm light), would he have achieved the sort of wide popularity that once belonged to Lord Peter Wimsey or Nero Wolfe?" (173). I would agree that it is not so much the warmth of the author's approach as the public's fascination with the rich and the powerful which makes even the antics of Shakespeare's aristocratic heros popular with American working-class students. As a teacher I can attest to that. Most of the blockbusters in literature have been about the rich and the powerful who leave their imprint, for good or ill, on a Hobbesian world. The biggest consumers of the TV soap opera *Dynasty*, for example, are lower middle- and working-class viewers who need to escape the drudgery of their own lives: Proletarians' revolutionary impulses are sublimated into the fantasy life of the rich and the famous. By contrast, Keating's heroes are resolute underdogs. The harried middle-class Ghote, the indomitable cockney Mrs. Craggs, even the Irish burglar in *A Remarkable Case of Burglary* are a refreshing departure from British novelists' preoccupation with upper-class concerns. With my own left-wing sympathies, I would like to think that this very anti-elitist thrust of Keating's fiction will make the literary establishment of the future pay attention to him. So that even if he does not become a money-spinner in life and after death as Christie continues to be, a future Barthes or a Derrida will train his critical guns on him as they have done on Fleming and Borghes.

The Ghote Novels

Writing in the tradition of English humanists like Graham Greene whom he so admires, Keating focuses the Ghote novels on the individual's power to retain his humanity within the rigid structures of law and order. He does so against the prevailing winds of post-modern theory blowing across the channel from France. While Barthes, Derrida, Foucault and Lacan have deconstructed the individual subject, the text and the author with Gallic wit and rigor, Keating's Ghote novels reaffirm the autonomy and authority of all three. It is Ghote's individual consciousness and its minutely observed complexities which bear the weight of Keating's philosophical explorations.

It is tempting to speculate that a little known book which Keating co-authored with his uncle, Maurice Keating, had a profound, if unacknowledged, influence on Keating. The book, *Understanding Teilhard de Chardin* was published five years after his first Ghote novel, but there is an odd similarity between de Chardin's theory of human consciousness and Keating's own portrayal of Ghote's inner musings. A Jesuit by training, and a competent paleontologist by choice, Teilhard's philosophy is notable for his synthesis of evolutionary biology, derived from Darwin, with his formulation of how man's consciousness evolved from his origins in the humble amoeba. While tracing the biological history of man in accordance with scientific facts, Teilhard emphasizes the importance of the origin, the growth and the complexity of man's interior life. According to Teilhard:

27

With the advent of the power of reflection everything is
changed. The phenomenon of man takes definite shape. The
cell becomes someone. After the grain of matter, the grain of
life, and then at last we see the grain of thought.

...What is spontaneously mental (or spiritual) is no longer an
aura round the physical; it becomes a principal part of the
phenomenon. (46-47)

In other words, Teilhard, sees man's power of reflection,
and his awareness of that power, as of primary
importance in his evolutionary history.

It is no wonder then that Keating's Ghote novels are
notable not for their fast-paced action or intricacy of plot
but for the complexity of his characters' interior lives. This
is particularly true of Keating's portrayal of Inspector
Ghote. The central paradox about Ghote is that while his
physical presence remains shadowy—we never learn what
he looks like—we come to know every shade, every
nuance of his feelings, be it his acute discomfort at the
overwhelming stridency of the American voice or his
embarrassment at being caught by his superior officer
giving money to an itinerant beggar. Keating is not above
devoting a whole page to every permutation of Ghote's
inner life, so that even though Ghote's physical presence
is elusive, his thoughts and feelings are brought vividly to
life.

Although Ghote is enshrined in the pantheon of great
detectives of literature—Otto Penzler has included an
essay by Keating on Ghote in his book *The Great
Detectives*—Ghote's very presence among the heroes of
detection like Sherlock Holmes, Lord Peter Wimsey and
Roderick Alleyn redefines the concept of greatness. For
great in the old traditional sense Ghote is most definitely
not. He does not command an imposing physical presence
like Holmes, nor is he aristocratic like Wimsey, nor *outre*
in appearance like Hercule Poirot. Not only is Ghote's
physical presence unprepossessing, even his intellect does

not inspire awe in the reader, his colleagues, or his wife. In fact, everyone Ghote meets tends to have the upper hand over him; he is a much put-upon man.

How then has Ghote managed to take his place among the colorful, showy, great detectives of tradition? Ghote is great simply because he is so intensely, ordinarily human. And that, in an increasingly dehumanized world, is no mean feat. Indeed, he redefines the meaning of greatness by his very lack of anything outstanding, anything heroic—for greatness, according to Keating, resides in being intensely human with all the heart-searching it implies. Indeed, if we agree with Teilhard de Chardin that consciousness is the measure of man, then Ghote, whose consciousness is exceptionally complex and constantly growing, exemplifies what it means to be human.

In his essay on Ghote, Keating assumes the point of view of a supposedly real inspector of Bombay Police who speculates, in his inimitable Indian English, on the authenticity of Ghote, "I am always wondering: is the fellow a real top-notch C.I.D. Inspector at all? Sometimes I am thinking he must be no more than an idea in the writer fellow's head" (112). With fiendish cleverness—a characteristic of most of his work—Keating goes on to reveal the genesis and development of Ghote's character through the irate speculations of the supposed inspector of police who is angry because Ghote gets all the best cases and gets sent abroad, regardless of his junior position.

What emerges from these speculations is that Ghote is as vague physically to his creator as he is to the reader. "Mr. Keating in the beginning saw a pair of shoulders only, thin and bony shoulders with a burden always upon them.... I do not believe the fellow altogether knows what like are Ghote's feet." Ghote's age, like his feet, is nebulous, and he has a son, Ved, who "has grown from five years to twelve only during the whole eleven-twelve years of Ghote's cases" (113). Then there is the question of

Ghote's wife, Protima, consistently described as beautiful and elegant, although how Ghote, a Mahrashtrian, came to have a Bengali wife is not explained. Also, Keating who has an uncanny ear for the comedy of Indian English, apparently came very close to committing an egregious blunder when he almost called Ghote, Ghosh—a Bengali name which "would be like saying that that so famous Commissaire Maigret of the Paris police force was called all the time Boris Ivanovitch" (114).

Ghote's adventures, both physical and mental, fleshes out Ghote's shadowy physical presence. What his physical description lacks in concrete detail is more than made up for by Keating's acute eye for the Indian landscape, both geographic and cultural, and his finely tuned ear for Indian speech patterns. In every Ghote novel, the climactic scene describes with vivid detail a uniquely Indian scene or event; for example, the first thunderstorm heralding the monsoon at the end of a long hot summer in *The Perfect Murder* and the colorful festival, Holi, in *Inspector Ghote's Good Crusade*. What is more remarkable, the scene functions as a dramatic turning point in Ghote's own psychological resolution.

Keating's ear for Indian English, which encompasses all the comic and epistemological possibilities inherent in it, enables him to register every vibration in Ghote's very intricate psyche. And it is this minutely detailed portrait of Ghote's inner life which makes Ghote so real and human. For example, how can we not identify with Ghote, not only in his specific Indianness but in his universal humanness when he agonizes over his cheap suitcase at Heathrow airport: "With a growing feeling of hot shame, he saw that every single piece of luggage that had so far appeared was infinitely more respectable in appearance than his big, light brown, rather cardboardy—no very cardboardy suitcase" (*Peacock* 8)? After an extended, very funny scene in which Ghote tries pathetically to avoid owning up to the cheap suitcase, but is finally forced to when the porter holds it up for all to see asking if the owner would come forward and identify it, Ghote has to face another humiliating contretemps. This time he finds that "his feet were being weepingly embraced" by the plump noisily emotional form of Vidur Datta who claims to be his "wife's cousin's husband" and who wants him to investigate the disappearance of his wife's beautiful and westernized niece known as the Peacock. Just when the scene is at its noisiest, a British bobby sent to receive the Indian representative to the Emergency Conference, the Smuggling Of Dangerous Drugs, accosts him. Ghote's humiliation is complete:

> But why, oh why, had Cousin Vidur chosen just the very moment when he was being sought out to make that ridiculous, undignified, over-emotional un-British scene? The constable could not but have heard and seen. At the very outset of the visit he had become a figure of fun. (*Peacock* 17)

What is involved here forms the underlying theme of the novel—Ghote's pathetic lack of self-assurance attributable both to the colonial heritage which has taught him that everything British (including their famed glacial persona) is necessarily superior, to his middle-class status which enables him to *recognize* but not *buy* quality things like a genuine leather suitcase. However, by the end of his stay in England during which he successfully investigates the disappearance of the Peacock, a case which even Scotland Yard had failed to solve, Ghote is disabused of his illusions about England. He finds that the real England, as opposed to his dreams of England based on readings in English literature, is as flawed as any other place in the world. Ghote's trip to England becomes one more voyage of discovery—of truth in its various, elusive forms.

One of the truths—the vindication of Ghote's essential integrity and humanness—is put to the test in every novel. Ghote receives a constant battering, because, although persistently and courageously human, he is constantly afraid of exposing his humanness in a society so bound by orthodoxy and bureaucracy that being human is perceived as a sign of weakness. The police force, of which Ghote is a diligent member, has to maintain the image of being tough, and Ghote is always afraid of being found too soft-hearted. Thus, in the opening chapter of *Inspector Ghote Trusts the Heart*, Ghote has just succumbed to the whiny machinations of a little beggar boy with a withered leg:

> He pulled out the two-paise piece and pressed it hastily, stealthily into the boy's thin-fleshed hard, little expectant hand. There. it was done.
>
> Freed of the burden, he swung sharply away and prepared to mount the steps at a trot.
>
> "Ah. It is Ghote. Inspector Ghote."
>
> A cold lurch of dismay froze him into stillness. Spotted. Found out. A hardhearted inspector of the Bombay C.I.D. seen falling for the totally transparent wiles of a mere boy of a beggar. (*Heart* 2)

However, as it turns out, the Commissioner of Police, who catches him in the act of giving money to a beggar, wants him for a special job for which Ghote's compassionate nature is precisely suited: "Inspector, this is a job that may well require the utmost tact. It needs a man of feeling. I saw you giving to that beggar boy as I drove up: I'm glad to find at least one of my officers hasn't let his duties rub away all the heart in him" (Heart 3).

The Commissioner wants Ghote to investigate a kidnapping in the household of his friend, a wealthy industrialist. The kidnapper, who had obviously intended to kidnap the industrialist's son for ransom, had, instead, taken a poor tailor's son by mistake, because the rich man's pampered son and the poor tailor's ragged little boy had exchanged their clothes when they played together.

The crux of the novel hinges on whether the poor tailor's son is dispensable, and therefore, should be used as a pawn in stern police measures to punish the kidnappers who would not hesitate to kill the boy if the industrialist did not pay ransom and called the police instead. Ghote has a doubly onerous task: he must induce the industrialist to dredge up the remnants of compassion unextinguished by his long ruthless financial climb and pay at least half the ransom asked for, and he must convince the Commissioner not to take drastic police action which would scare the kidnappers into killing the boy. His task is further complicated by the uxorious industrialist's beautiful and greedy young wife, who is loathe to see one paise of her husband's money go to succor the poor, and who uses all her sexual wiles to harden her husband's heart.

The industrialist vacillates between compassion and rationalization, but finally, the Commissioner's and his wife's counsel to leave it all to the police and deny ransom prevails. Ghote is dismissed from the case. However, in the middle of his professional and personal defeat, he has a blinding insight about the location of the kidnappers (no mean task in the teeming city of Bombay) and decides to follow up the clue on his own. He finds the kidnapped boy—a starved, filthy, apathetic, barely breathing huddle of bones. At this exact moment, the Commissioner appears, successful in his own ruthless, efficient methods, and rewards Ghote for his intelligence and disinterested humanitarianism, by sending him up against the Disciplinary Board for insubordination: "Nobody, Inspector, nobody slides out of obeying orders I give him and then goes off on his own sticking his dirty little fingers into my case" (*Heart* 200).

The Commissioner's attitude—punishing Ghote for insubordination rather than rewarding him for "trusting his heart" and showing his initiative—devastates Ghote.

But again, what provides a catharsis for the novel and personal redemption for Ghote are brief flashes of human contact. In the middle of arresting the kidnappers, Ghote manages to buy a bobbing red balloon and put it in the hand of the little boy in an attempt to rouse him from his apathy. The Commissioner's rigidity is contrasted to little Pidku's flicker of life nurtured by Ghote's wonderful understanding of the child's needs:

> He took Ghote's mute burden from him with stiff precision, turned and walked smartly out into the street, the red balloon still clutched in Pidku's hand bobbing and bouncing absurdly about him. Outside the proprietor of Trust X stood with the old tailor, the richly suited tall figure and the lean-shanked, single-darned one side by side. As the ambulance driver waited for his companion to open the back door of their vehicle, Ghote saw the tailor put out a tentative hand to his son and gently touch him. And then at last Pidku smiled.
>
> * * *
>
> Ghote felt his lethargic gloom sliding away like great, stiff cakes of dust under the first rain of the monsoon. (*Heart* 200-201)

Over and over again, Keating makes the point that humanness consists not in following abstractions, bureaucratic or philosophical, but in one individual confronting another and doing his duty by the other. As the wealthy proprietor of Trust X explains his decision to pay the ransom for the tailor's boy: "It is that I have spoken to the father. He and I have spoken face to face. I must pay. I will pay" (*Heart* 69).

In *Inspector Ghote's Good Crusade*, this theme is set in the context of a larger, very current subject—American philanthropy. An American millionaire, Frank Masters, who has set up a Foundation for the care of juvenile vagrants in the city of Bombay and who is described by everyone as a good man, is murdered. No one can understand the motive for his murder—a quantity of arsenic has supposedly been slipped into the meal he has eaten.

The novel shows Ghote's deductive powers turning into sentimental mush by his admiration for Master's philanthropy. Wonderful comedy follows as Ghote, neglecting his real duty—that of investigating the murder—attempts to emulate Master's philanthropy by giving five hundred rupees, saved over many months in order to buy his wife a much needed refrigerator, to a fisherman's paramour who spins him a tale of woe. When Ghote looks back at the woman, "It came as no real surprise to see that the enormous paramour was sitting visibly quivering, even at this distance, with great tides of irrepressible laughter" (*Crusade* 186).

Not only is the paramour overcome with hilarity at Ghote's gullibility, she spends all the money not on paying off her debts, but on a riotous festival—Holi. This great, rambunctious, Bacchanalian festival, as anthropologists have shown, is designed to reverse conventional social hierarchy. In the colorful free-for-all of this festival, license is granted to generally humiliate those in power. Ghote, appropriately enough as the prime representative of the law, is gleefully pounced on by the revellers:

> Tossing powder by the handful, squirting ink by the bicycle pumpful, they came at him from every side. In seconds he was red wet, blue wet, yellow wet. And on to the wetness the coloured powders, pink, turquoise, and orange, clung and smeared...I have deserved this he thought. This is a fit punishment for coming here with my money and telling people how to live their lives. Exactly fit. (*Crusade* 226)

This insight into the arrogance inherent in philanthropy helps him to knock Masters off his saintly pedestal and to see clearly that he was a fallible human being; it also gives him a further insight into the motive for the murder. From finding the motive to finding the murderer proves a short, logical step.

That perfection is incompatible with being fully human is a theme most fully and comically explored in Keating's first Ghote novel, *The Perfect Murder*. As Keating explains: "whether you should strive to be perfect, or whether you should settle for the halfway, applies in even the smallest things in life. You're typing a sheet of paper and make one mistake; do you rip it out of the typewriter, or do you erase the error?" (*The Great Detectives* 110). Keating's choice of locale is perfect for the exploration of this theme, for where else but in India, so monumentally imperfect and so indubitably human could you sound all the variations on this theme? If Keating had set this theme in super-efficient Germany, for example, he would have run into trouble. What is remarkable about this novel is that Keating pulls off every blatantly farcical device to reinforce his theme. For example, when Ghote is sent to investigate a murder which has splattered headlines over every newspaper as "The Perfect Murder," he finds that the murder is far from perfect—it is a botched up affair and the victim named Perfect, secretary to a gross, wealthy businessman, Lala Varde, is alive though concussed and unconscious.

If Ghote, a diligent student of Hans Gross' *Criminal Investigation*, expects to apply the rigorous investigative methods of Scotland Yard of which he is colonial heir, he is quickly disillusioned. No one cooperates with Ghote. Lala Varde considers that his enormous wealth places him above the obligations of ordinary citizens; his spoiled sons, Dilip and Prem, and his fearfully imposing wife, Laxmi, obstruct Ghote at every step for their own devious reasons. As if all this obstreperousness were not enough, Ghote is entrusted with another case—a laughable one concerning the disappearance of one rupee (about 11 cents) from an austere minister's desk.

The final straw that threatens to break poor Ghote's bony back is the fact that a big Swede, Axel Svenson, from UNESCO, attaches himself to Ghote in order to study Indian police methods. Svenson blunders after Ghote like a bumbling St. Bernard, adding to Ghote's problems, but a genuine friendship develops between them when Ghote risks being a little late for an appointment with the fanatically punctual Minister for Police Affairs in order to help Svenson—thus once again putting humanness above an abstract idea. Nature plays its own inexorable role, adding to the general muddle in India: a heatwave is on, a prelude to the spectacular tropical thunderstorm which, when it breaks, clears the muddle in Ghote's own mind, and helps him, in a burst of brilliant insight, to solve the case. The solution, like the crime, is absurd in its imperfection, but the very imperfection is responsible for saving a life.

In *Inspector Ghote Goes by Train*, the other facet of perfection is portrayed—arrogance, playful self-assertion turning to anarchist villainy and disruption of the social order. Ghote is sent to Calcutta to nab the master criminal A.K. Bhattacharya, who has amassed a fortune by selling fake antiques. By choosing to travel by the slow, humble train when he was empowered to fly, Ghote is the opposite of the mythical Icarus who flies too close to the sun and is burnt for his pains. As he explains to the scornful, disguised Bhattacharya who sits opposite him and baits him unmercifully: "That is what is wrong. I tell you it is wrong. Wrong to go so high, wrong to like to see so much wrong, wrong" (*Train* 20). Bhattacharya's reply brings the classical motif underlying the novel to the forefront: "You cannot be meaning to tell me that you equate the simple act of travelling by air with the presumption of Icarus?" (*Train* 20).

In *Goes by Train* Keating again manages to integrate a characteristic feature of the Indian scene—travel by train—

with philosophical concerns and the form of a suspense novel. *Goes by Train*, however, departs from an orthodox whodunit in the fact that the identity of the criminal is known. Although Ghote initially has trouble identifying him positively as the man he wants, halfway through the novel the criminal reveals his true identity in a characteristic moment of hubris. The rest of the novel becomes a duel of wits. All the people in Ghote's compartment are stuck with one another for the duration of the train journey, and this allows Keating to draw a comic picture of two American hippies, Red and Mary Jane, their guru and Mr. Ramaswamy from Madras whose inimitable accent—he prefaces every word with an "e" (for example, "e-Sir")—Keating catches with great accuracy. The characterization is neither subtle or deep. All the travelers with the exception of Ghote and Bhattacharya are stereotypes, but they are great fun, and Keating satirizes stock types with gusto. Besides evoking the claustrophobic intimacy and the illusion of timelessness which train travel induces, Keating has a marvelous chase scene, reminiscent of Hitchcock, in which Ghote chases Bhattacharya over the roof of the train—a scene which provides a thrilling climax to the novel.

Ghote, as usual, is subjected to every humiliation and near defeat: he nearly dies of opium poisoning; Bhattacharya continually and cruelly baits him; and in a macabre scene, a one-eyed barber at a wayside station (bribed by Bhattacharya) holds Ghote helpless by his nose while he brandishes a knife, nearly causing Ghote to miss the train and lose the villain. Of course, Ghote emerges modestly triumphant at the end, his integrity and humanity intact. For unlike his fellow officers, Ghote never uses third degree methods nor does he use torture to extract confessions from even the most brutal suspects. Ghote's unfailing weapons are his patience and persistence. Even the most hardened criminal who has withstood the sadistic Inspector Phadke's torture gives in to Ghote's quiet determination. Even Bhattacharya's will, so strong, so arrogant, breaks down before Ghote's determination, and he makes a long and detailed confession of his fraudulent dealings.

From where do Ghote's infinite patience and persistence come? They come from the fact that in spite of the constant humiliation he suffers, in spite of his comic bumbling, in spite of the fact that his superior officers and even his charming wife constantly bully him, Ghote manages to do his duty by his job, by his family, and those around him. Confronted by an investigative problem or a human contretemps, Ghote, with a quiet, deceptive stubbornness, never gives up. Like a dog worrying a bone, Ghote keeps at it till the problem yields a solution.

A very clearly defined sense of duty leads Ghote in *Inspector Ghote Breaks an Egg* to redefine himself in a way which lifts him above a specific Indian context to a larger, universal one. In India, Hinduism, the predominant religion of the country, defines every individual according to an intricate hierarchy of caste and family distinctions. Self-definition according to one's work is a recent acquisition. In the traditional Indian context, loyalty to one's family and caste is placed above loyalty to the state. Ghote's investigation of a possible murder committed 15 years earlier takes him to a remote Indian village where inherited values fight a vigorous battle before yielding to new, Western ones.

As the title indicates, the *deus ex machina* is a brightly colored box of eggs. Because the suspected murderer is the powerful Municipal Chairman who keeps the village in order with his personal band of hoods, Ghote has been ordered to disguise himself as a chicken feed salesman advertising a new company: "Grofat Chicken Feeds, Ltd." As the eminent political figure who orders the investigation tells him, "The average size of the Indian egg, did you know, is disgraceful as compared with the American and British egg. It's nothing less, indeed, than a national disaster" (*Egg* 2). The eminent figure, it turns out, is concerned not so much with the national disaster as with promoting his nephew's interests—the nephew owns the factory manufacturing the chicken feed. From the beginning, Keating sets the comic tone of the novel— Indians' perennial conflict between the personal and the public, between the old and the new fought out in terms of the absurd, a box of eggs. Absurd and trivial as it may be, the box of eggs plays a crucial role in the violence charged climax of the novel.

After a great deal of agonized self-questioning, Ghote has to decide what his values are and where his loyalties should lie. The test comes when Ghote is ordered to drop the investigation when he is very close to the truth. The eminent figure is not interested in truth; he is interested only in discrediting the wealthy, powerful Municipal Chairman so that his clout in party politics is undercut. As he tells Ghote, it is not necessary to find out if the Chairman poisoned his first wife because the discovery that the Chairman is really the son of a Harijan beggar woman, and not a Brahmin as he has passed himself off, is enough to destroy him. For in caste-ridden India, the mere fact of being an untouchable has terrible consequences, and that is enough to destroy the Chairman. However, Ghote "knew that he would not have been able to live with the thought of abandoning a case of murder at the whim of a politician when the whole case was within hours of being satisfactorily completed. His whole reason for existence would have been crumbled up to fragments inside him" (*Egg* 164). Ghote's awareness that his reason for existence lies in his pursuit of truth as his job dictates, marks him out as a human being able to choose and accept the risks and responsibilities of that choice.

Ghote's heroism stems not so much from spectacular encounters with danger and death, from shooting from the hip, or jumping off cliffs *a la* James Bond, but in quietly and stubbornly attending to and completing the task immediately at hand. In *Breaks an Egg* for example, Ghote takes a few precious minutes off to talk a troubled adolescent out of drowning himself. Ghote is surrounded by the Chairman's hired thugs and a few minutes spent talking to the boy might cost him his life: "But in front of him was a tormented young man, and it was more than probable that his torment was one of the self-inflicted ones of youth. Ghote addressed himself to the immediate task again" (82).

Doing what has to be done, Ghote braves the incandescent wrath of a holyman who has begun a fast unto death to oppose the government investigation of the Chairman. In a country as remorselessly religious as India, the holyman's death, construed as martyrdom, might cause a riot. Ghote commits an egregious *faux pas* by bringing into the sacred precincts of the temple a box of eggs. The swami explodes at Ghote: "It is carried to disgust me... Well you are knowing that the egg is equally forbidden to pass the lips as any meat. And into this temple you bring them. Go. Go now. Go this instant. Or I will curse you" (*Egg* 60). However, when the holyman is on the point of death, Ghote does not hesitate to force the whites from the despised egg down his throat and revive him with the help of the fortunately "irreligious Sikh" doctor. In the extended and wholly believable descriptions of the confrontation between Ghote and the Swami, Keating accomplishes three things with masterly economy: he etches in one more fine point about Ghote's heroic persistence and pragmatism; he illustrates the everpresent conflict between the spiritual and the secular India, and finally the box of eggs comically vindicates its existence as a *deus ex machina*.

Another novel in which the form and theme are beautifully woven together is *Bats Fly Up for Inspector Ghote*. BATS happens to be the acronym for the Black Money and Allied Transaction Squad—a band of elite police officers assigned to fight the extensive circulation of black money made from smuggled and illegally sold gold. Real bats, black with outstretched wings, swoop down on the city of Bombay heralding the darkness which shelters the pick pockets. Bats also rest in the banana tree in Ghote's backyard and destroy the green bananas Ghote hopes will ripen soon. Bats of suspicion and jealousy flit around and cloud Ghote's mind as his wife, Protima, constantly praises Inspector Rhadwan, the dashing Moslem member of the BATS. Rhadwan who has moved in as Ghote's neighbor is gallant to Protima and is rich enough to send his ailing wife to an expensive resort town. He is also, as Protima never fails to point out, home much more than Ghote is. In addition to his sense of all these shortcomings, Ghote's mind is tainted by the constant suspicion he has to direct against his colleagues—he has the job of nosing out the traitor among his colleagues who is serving as an informer, for the blackmarketeers always manage to elude the net cast for their capture. Surely one of the BATS is a traitor.

The climax is reached in a nice blending of the professional and domestic. Their quarry has once again escaped the elaborate and super efficient schemes laid by the BATS, and Ghote is no wiser about the identity of the traitor. All five members of the Squad seem equally innocent or guilty. His preoccupation with the case has made Ghote neglect his wife, Protima, and son, Ved. They are resentful of him and he is suspicious of them—a carry-over from his profession. The domestic kettle boils over when Ghote quite unjustifiably suspects little Ved of stealing money. Ved bursts into tears. Protima is furious. Ghote feels a failure, as a detective, as a father and as a husband. Realizing that his mind is so tainted with suspicion that it is in danger of becoming quite unhinged, he decides to resign from his job. Coming home tired and dispirited, Protima's taunts about how the dashing Rhadwan dealt efficiently with the bats ignite the last embers of his courage. Risking his life, he climbs the tree, dislodges the bats and sustains a fall. The fall, however, turns out to be fortunate—a forgotten wallet which he confiscated a long time ago from a pickpocket drops out of his pocket. Protima's tenderness and solicitude over his fall and her faith that he will, with his superior intelligence, be able to find the owner of the wallet among the teeming millions of Bombay, dissipates the fog of jealousy and suspicion which had clouded his mind and prevented him from seeing the truth. He solves the case in a burst of brilliant intuition, and, in a final scene in the Natural History Section of the Prince of Wales Museum, lays bare the culprit. On his way out, he halts before a painting of a forest scene:

> In the jungle round a forest pool in Assam, two tigers were crouched drinking. But it was not on these powerful and sleek forms that Inspector Ghote's gaze came to rest. It fixed, instead, on one tiny characteristic detail that the artist had incorporated in their scene. Up in the shadowed branches of one of the trees overhanging the pool there had cunningly been placed the stuffed bodies of a cluster of bats. And they were deep and safely in their noonday sleep. (180)

Keating has claimed that he wrote the first ten Ghote books before he ever went to India. He visited India briefly in 1974 and 1975, the second time invited by the BBC which had made a movie on Ghote. Perhaps inspired by these visits, his post-India novel published in 1976, *Filmi, Filmi Inspector Ghote* deals with the murder of an Indian actor in a Bombay film studio. The book is the least subtle of the Ghote books. It is tempting to speculate that Keating's contact with India in its most tinsellish aspect— the Bombay film world which Keating, with heavy handed satire, terms Bollywood—has prevented him from exercising the detachment so necessary for the creative imagination. The truth of Keating's satire of the Bombay film world cannot be disputed, but it is too easy and self evident a truth. Bollywood is, even to the most star-struck dimwit, a sleezier, stupider Hollywood, if that can be imagined, and, as Horatio would say, it needs "no ghost...come from the grave to tell us this." Keating's knowledge of the Indian social hierarchy: for example, the fact that hangers-on of public figures are called chamchas, spoons, is again on display here, but all the characters are cardboard or rather, celluloid, figures. Even the Bombay film version of *Macbeth* as Maqbet is funny only at the level of slapstick, not at the level of the subtle comedy of earlier books.

When Keating relies on his fertile imagination to flesh out India's colonial past as he does in *Murder of a Maharajah*, he excels. Maharajah is not strictly a Ghote novel, though there is a diabolically clever link established with Ghote at the end, but I shall consider it a Ghote novel. It is set in the 1930s during the heyday of British rule when despotic maharajahs spent much of their time organizing spectacular tiger shoots and entertaining their British overlords in a style to which they were *not* accustomed.

The central figure, the Maharajah, as in most orthodox whodunits, is both the prime mover of the plot and the victim. He is also a believable character, both as a stereotypical tyrant and as a complex human being minimally attractive because of his appetite for life and wholly repulsive because of his all-consuming ego. His ego will brook no opposition when it is suggested by an American engineer that the dam he built for millions of dollars should be used to irrigate vast areas of land lying arid and useless to his starving subjects. The Maharajah refuses to put the dam into use for fear that the water level in the lake used by the sandgrouse will go down too low to attract the birds and ruin his favorite sport— sandgrouse shooting.

The novel begins with a bit of arcane folklore of sufficient interest to involve the reader's attention immediately. A humble villager is on his way to the

Maharajah's palace to present him with a rare tribute—a piece of Sapura bark which grows on a tree once in a hundred years, and which has the even rarer attribute of stiffening into the hardness of iron when it comes into contact with water and coloring everything it touches with an indelible orange dye. Both these properties are crucial to the development and resolution of the plot.

As a counterpoint to this piece of ancient folklore, there is a thoroughly modern, thoroughly enjoyable contrivance—the Maharajah's favorite toy, a huge silver electric train which runs around the dining table carrying delectable deserts and liqueurs, all listed with an almost medieval relish in enumerating gastronomic delights. Not content with playing a perfectly infantile joke on little Michael, the Resident's son, on April Fool's Day, the Maharajah uses the train to play a joke on one of his 12 (Last Supper?) dinner guests. As Henry Morton III reaches over to one of the silver carriages to help himself to a bottle of creme de cacao, a hidden spring sends the bottle shooting up, spraying a "thick stream of dark chocolaty, sticky liquid all over him." Henry Morton, the "soft metals king of the American midwest" who had been summoned to reopen negotiations on the zinc-mining in Bhopore becomes the last victim of the Maharajah's April Fool's Day jokes.

The Maharajah's first victim, little Michael, is about to get into his chauffeur-driven Rolls after a protracted and difficult audience with the Maharajah when there is an explosion—the exhaust is found to be blocked by a piece of Sapura bark. These two practical jokes turn against the Maharajah in a distinctly unfunny way and cost him his life. Someone, taking a lesson from the Maharajah's macabre ingenuity, stuffs the Maharajah's gun with a piece of bark, so that during the sandgrouse shoot the next morning it explodes in his face and kills him.

The excitement, the primitive thrill of the sandgrouse shoot in the beautiful light of an Indian dawn is vividly described:

Then, quite suddenly, the sky on its first tinge of pink-red. And the whole huge dome of the heavens above, which when they had set out had still been pricked with pale stars, moved imperceptibly from blue-black to an overarching pallor. The shape of the land round the unmoving water of the lakes began to be just discernable.

And then, after a single long hush, the first heralds of the sandgrouse could be heard as a tiny insistent drumming of wings. (76)

Even if one were not a fan of detective fiction, *Maharajah* would be worth reading as a satirical evocation of India's colonial past. Keating juxtaposes, with tongue-in-cheek irony, the beauty of the well orchestrated hunt and the appalling cruelty to the poor on which it rests. As mentioned earlier, the water level in the *jheel* which attracts the birds is maintained by denying the peasants the use of the dam which they have built at enormous cost and hard labor. The peasants are denied water so that the sandgrouse may drink and be shot.

The man summoned by the Resident to investigate the murder of the Maharajah is District Superintendent of Police Howard who despite his "remarkable record of successes" is regrettably "country born":

To be "countryborn," not to have been subjected, if by chance your actual birth had occurred in India, to the bracing climate of the mother country, that climate that was always thought of as being not simply physically bracing with its cold winds, its hard driving rain, its pure snows, but also being morally bracing. A man who had not had that was somehow suspect. (93)

Keating's understanding of the intricacies of colonial snobbery adds one more dimension to the book, and makes D.S.P. Howard an interesting figure who, as a social outcast, belongs nowhere and yet is at home everywhere. He plays tennis with his ultra-British Resident, whose often reiterated advice to his son to "keep your mouth shut and your bowels open" surely epitomizes the moral atavism on which imperialism rests, and he is at home with the Maharajah's circle and can befriend on equal terms the austere, acute schoolmaster who serves as his sidekick in the investigation.

The investigation itself turns out to be unexpectedly tricky. All 12 of the Maharajah's guests have equally strong motives for murdering the host: the son and heir, the new Maharajah, whose love for Dolly Brattle, an aging chorus girl, had been contemptuously dismissed by his father who had urged him to marry a princess and keep Dolly where she belongs—in a harem; Joe Lloyd, the fiery engineer, whose dam lay useless because of the old Maharajah's whim; Dolly, whose brassy blonde person was not proof against the Maharajah's insults; and Henry Morton, who had been summoned all the way from the Midwest only to be made a fool of. In this novel, as D.S.P. Howard and the schoolmaster explore the palace and the motives of its guests for clues to murder, Keating manages to avoid the tediousness often present in his and in other redoubtable whodunits of the investigative process—the patient questioning, the elaborate mathematical juggling of clues, timetables and alibis. The uncovering of the clues also becomes an exposé of a way of life so exotic, so grotesquely splendid, that the novel holds the reader's interest from first to last. It is also, unlike conventional "period" novels which tend to take themselves too seriously, utterly playful, and, therefore, unpretentious and delightful. And playfulness is and should be a feature of the whodunit as it is, above all, a puzzle which *Homo Ludens* likes to solve when he is not trying, with his usual lack of success, to solve the mystery of existence.

In a letter to me Keating professes to be surprised at the success of *Maharajah* which he terms, rather dismissively, a "conventional mystery": "I did it at what I thought was a good deal more superficial a level and to my embarrassment my editor liked it more than anything I had done." Ironically, Keating's most superficial novels are *Filmi, Filmi Inspector Ghote,* and *Go West Inspector Ghote,* both written after brief contacts with the reality they try to depict, and both lacking the panache which distinguishes *Maharajah,* written from a considerable distance in time and place. Indeed, Keating's brush with reality, whether it be dusty and dirty Bombay or the plastic and shiny Los Angeles, seems to hamper his inventive powers, for like *Filmi, Filmi, Go West* is rather superficial and contrived. As in all Ghote novels, Keating explores an interesting theme—the export of instant Indian spirituality to the West. Ghote is sent to Los Angeles to bring back the only daughter of a Bombay businessman who has dropped out of college in California to join the Ashram of an Indian Swami. Keating's portrayal of the Swami, who recalls Jim Jones who led hundreds of people to suicide in Guyana in the absolute charismatic power he wields over his mindless followers, is unerringly accurate. He is also very good at portraying Ghote's bemused response to the stridency of the American scene, but the kind of depth of understanding he reveals in his portrayal of Indian village politics in *Breaks an Egg* is missing here, and the solution to the murder is contrived and implausible.

While Keating does not try to delve into the question of why the devotees of these so-called spiritual leaders behave like half-witted sheep, the Swami himself comes alive in all his complexity. Incipient sadist, blatant lecher and complete fraud that the Swami is, Keating, however, entertains the possibility that there are more things in heaven and earth than are dreamt of in our super-rational age. As Ghote puts it, "events do occur which can be called magic events which cannot be accounted for by logical, scientific means" (*West* 75). Demonstrating his power, the Swami singles Ghote out in a vast crowd as "someone who has come and is not happy. His head is paining. He needs help. You there, at the back of the doors, come here to me" (32). Indeed, Ghote ever since he has landed in California, has been suffering from a throbbing head. Reluctantly he goes up to the Swami who puts his right hand on his shoulder:

> Ghote at once felt a sensation of peculiar warmth there...It was as if, he felt, there was an actual source of heat within that dense, soft flesh. And immediately as the weariness and grittiness accumulated over hours of being swept through the skies at hundreds of miles an hour began seeping out of him through it seemed, some sump-hole in the back of his neck...Damn him. Why should he be endowed with a power like this? (33-34)

While one must admire Keating's open-minded attitude to the mystery of spiritual powers, his explanations of the Swami's final degradation as voiced by Johananda, a believable observer, is far too facile: "When he came out here to California first he was a truly God-realized person. A true yogi. But, you know, one of the great masters once said that everything on this earth is like a mingling of sand and sugar. But, poor Swami, after a while he began to think that California sand was sweeter than sugar" (175). Keating takes the easy way out; instead of tackling the difficult subject of the authenticity or inauthenticity of Indian mysticism, or ignoring the subject because it may be too large for the scope of a detective novel, he "solves" the problem, as it were, by blaming the potential for corruption inherent in it on the influence of the West. It boils down to that old chestnut—the West is materialistic, the East is spiritual. Why the West is so anxious to exchange its relatively solid dollar for the essentially light weight brand of spirituality exported from the East may not be as easily solved as the Swami's murder.

It should be obvious from this survey of Keating's Ghote novels that his philosophical and satirical themes have immense variety. What gives authenticity to this approach, and prevents the unpretentious whodunit form from sinking under the philosophical freight it carries, is his unfailing comic vision conveyed chiefly through his mastery of Indian English. The comedy springs from the fact that Indian English is the result of an uneasy marriage between a world view handed down from India's Vedic past and an essentially alien, even inimical, structure of thought embodied in the English language. For in this post-Wittgenstein and post-structuralist era we know that language, far from representing reality, shapes and reconstructs reality according to the demands of its inherent order and the values and assumptions of the people who use it. Much of the comedy of Indian English springs from the fact that the English language, homegrown over centuries in the sceptered isle, was roughly grafted to an entirely different culture in an entirely different climate.

This rough grafting has produced innumerable saplings. For apart from its political unity (imposed by the British) India is not really one country; rather, it is a loose federation of states each of which has a distinct linguistic, ethnic and cultural character, all reflected in the syntax and rhythms of its English. For example, a Northerner and a Southerner (and their sub-varieties) can immediately identify the region the other comes from by the accent and structure of the English he speaks. And ironically they can communicate only in English, for although Hindi has been declared the national language of India, Southerners refuse to learn it because they see Hindi, the language of the North, as an instrument of domination. For all intents and purposes, even after nearly forty years of independence from British rule, English remains the national language of India.

In addition to the varieties of English spoken by different ethnic groups, there are variations created by differences in economic class and education. Roughly, there are three kinds of English spoken in India which reflect a person's economic and educational background. They are the monosyllabic sentence fragments consisting mostly of verbs and nouns spoken by taxi drivers, waiters and others who deal with those economically better off than themselves; the fluent English spoken by those who have attended vocational and professional colleges which, however, bears the imprint of their regional language in its grammar, syntax and accent; the idiomatic, almost British English lightly spiced with a distinctively Indian lilt spoken by westernized Indians who have degrees in the humanities. There are many other variations, of course, but these three categories provide a convenient way of dealing with the social framework of Keating's novels.

Ghote is a police officer trained in the British judicial system, and his English is representative of the second category. Whenever his professional ethics show signs of weakening, he fortifies himself with a glance at his Bible— Han Gross' *Criminal Investigation*. The chief characteristic of Ghote's English is the use of a present participle without its object. For example, in *Breaks an Egg*, when an old woman drops a *Time* magazine, Ghote picks it up and delays handing it back because a picture of himself has caught his eye. The woman screams "Mine, mine," and Ghote reassures her with, "Yes, yes, I am giving" (4). Keating does not make it clear whether this exchange is in one of the Indian languages, or in English. It does not matter. Ghote's reply catches the authentic flavor of the syntax of an Indian language and the way it is transferred to English. The encounter between the local Superintendent of Police and Inspector Ghote further illustrates Keating's grasp of all the nuances of Indian English. When Ghote demands a room to work in, the Superintendent replies: "Very well, my dear fellow, if you are insisting, I will see that it is done. But we are faced with a problem here, I do not mind telling" (16). Once again, we notice the use of the participle "insisting" instead of the verb "insist." Also, the Superintendent transforms the phrase "I must confess" into its Indianized version "I do not mind telling." Ghote also drops his articles when he asks about the state of the prison cells: "Are they in dirty condition?" (16). Ghote often sounds stiffly formal because, lacking idiomatic ease in English, he uses the jargon of bureaucracy; "Then shall we go and select one as office for me? ...And perhaps you could see that a stronger-than-regulation bulb is found for it. I expect I shall be working all night" (16).

This Indianization of the structure of English indicates something very important: the Indianization of Western epistemology. A good example is the use of a present participle for a transitive verb. The average Indian's inability to use a past perfect or future perfect verb, his reliance on the present participle, reflects his attitude to time—he finds it hard to grasp a linear, historical time segmented into a past, present and future. (I shudder at my generalizations. Is there such a persona as an average Indian or an average Englishman? But, for the purpose of this analysis, I have to make these generalizations and risk becoming formulaic and reductive.) He lives in an eternal present, the *now* of mythical time which in T.S. Eliot's words "contains a time past and a time future." The Indian concept of reincarnation perceives life as an endlessly recurring cycle of existence on earth, a cycle you can bring to a halt only if you dissolve your individual soul, your *Atman*, into the universal soul—the *Brahman*. Death does not, as in the West, cut you off forever from life on earth. All the *carpe diem* in the lyrics of the seventeenth-century English poets dwells on this brevity of human life on earth unconsoled by the promise of continued life in heaven or hell or purgatory. There is no sense of urgency in an Indian's attitude to life because he has the assurance that he will taste its pleasures over and over again.

If Ghote's English reveals the remnants of Hindu epistemology clinging to the rough and ready translation of his thoughts from a native idiom to an alien one, there is the even funnier English spoken by the street urchins of Bombay. Born and bred on the teeming streets of that cosmopolitan city, these delinquents manage to cope with the appalling cruelty of their existence by taking refuge in the fantasy world of Hollywood movies. The leader of a gang who has "the head of a twelve-year-old boy and the face of a man of sixty" because of "the spread of some sort of infection which had crinkled the skin of the boy's face into a thousand etched tortuous lines" (*Crusade* 11) calls himself Edward G. Robinson. The boy is so streetwise, so distrustful of authority that Ghote is continually foiled in his attempts to extract information from him. It is only when Ghote, with characteristic insight, realizes that if he resorts to the boy's old Hollywood idiom he might be able to break down the boy's resistance, that things begin to move. What follows is an extremely funny, yet pathetic dialogue:

> "Nah," he [the boy] said, "When I keep watch on a fella he don't know there's nothing there."
> "Smart guy," Ghote said. "You gonna say what this fella did?"
> "Maybe."
> "Fill you full o' lead if you don't." (*Crusade* 63)

The farcical humor of the dialogue springs, of course, from the encroachment of Hollywood tinsel glitter into the slums of Bombay. But these incongruous fantasies also enable these poor naked forked animals to survive in a world where they are indeed as flies to the wanton gods.

At the other end of the social scale are the Westernized, upper-class Indians who are not Hindu, and who, therefore, speak an ultra British, though comically dated, English. Here is an "irreligious Sikh": "Give me a hand, old boy, and we will have something in him in a jiffy. We'd better mix it with a bit of water, digests easier that way..." (*Egg* 170). The Sikh punctuates his sentences with "old boy," "jiffy," "old chap" in the best Colonel Blimp manner. Then there is an amazingly believable portrait of a judge, a Moslem, who though retired and almost a recluse, does not bend an inch from his former eminence, and whose antediluvian attitudes are revealed in the precise cadences of his speech: "I had allowed myself to hope that the plain expression of plain facts, however few the ears that heard them, would do some good in these dark times, that with lies and corruption all around us a few grains of truth would show up like specks of white in the universal blackness" (*Line* 29). The antithesis of an aristocratic Moslem judge is a South Indian Brahmin, Mr. Ramaswamy, a mere cog in the vast bureaucratic machinery. Mr. Ramaswamy's speech with, as Ghote is quick to note, its "intrusive 'e' in front of words beginning with an 's' " (*Train* 78), marks him out as a Southerner, and the futility of his profession is conveyed perfectly in the windy formality of his speech:

> That is precisely the nature of my occupation. I travel all around the area of the Central Railway and sometimes make forays into other areas, and e-Sir, I inspect the forms kept at my station I choose to descend upon. And, of course, the stationary. It is, you will agree, a curious form of existence. (81)

In *Go West Ghote*, Keating catches the exact cadences of the dangerously manipulative rhetoric that flows from the bogus Guru and engulfs the audience like warm treacle:

> My friends, today I have something to give to you. A present from Swami. Is it a little, little present? Oh no. Swami is feeling very kind. He is going to give each of you a present that is very, very valuable. It is a present that he knew he was going to give long, long ago when he was meditating in the Himalayas and an inner command came to him that said: Go West, young man, go West. Yes, Swami is

going to give you now—a future. It will be a future guarded more wisely than your future ever could be by an insurance company however, careful. Yes, I am giving it.... (35)

Keating's next novel, *The Sheriff of Bombay*, published in 1984, nearly three years after *Go West Ghote*, takes us to a very different milieu. From affluent California where the children of the rich seek spiritual sustenance at the feet of spurious "gurus," we move to the sordid streets of the red-light district of Bombay where sex is bought and sold and where women and children are forced to sell their bodies by the unbearable cruelty of their circumstances.

Ghote is landed with a crime in this unlovely locale by the Assistant Commissioner of Police. The philosophical conundrum on which the novel rests is sounded right in the beginning when Ghote is on his way to answer the Assistant Commissioner of Police's peremptory summons. He is accosted by the anachronistic Anglo-Indian inspector D'Sa who holds one of those plastic covered "trick" pictures he had confiscated, with a great deal of righteous indignation, near the police station. From one angle, the picture is of a young woman wearing a red skirt and blue blouse. A slight turn of the wrist and the picture is of a naked girl. D'Sa, who lives in a rose colored British past, fulminates against modern decadence while simultaneously bemoaning the passing of the "upright" British order. This little incident neatly captures two of the main themes of the novel: one an exploration, almost sociological in its unsentimental realism, of the world of prostitution and the other, the theme of point of view:

It was all a matter of looking at things from one point of view or another. Like that dreadful book of Ved's Protima had found. One moment a disgusting sex manual, the next a *Boys and Girls Book of Facts*. One moment apparently crammed with pieces of useful information, the next a mishmash of inaccuracies. A transformation. (166)

It turns out that the ACP has summoned him not to hand him a "major inquiry" as he had hoped, but to act as a tour guide to a once famous, but now aging British film star, hero-worshipped in India as the swashbuckler or more accurately as the svashbuckler. Ghote's hopes immediately perk up, "To show him all the best of Bombay. It was hardly a first-class murder inquiry, but it was an honour all the same" (5). They are dashed immediately by the ACP's next words, "Chap wants to see the cages, Inspector" (5). Ghote, of course, is disillusioned. He muses inwardly, "For the Svashbuckler to be taken to see them. For such a hero. Such a white man. Such a god. It was not at all the right thing" (6). The cages are "notorious brothels that were at once Bombay's boast and its shame" (5).

Ghote's first meeting with the Swashbuckler turns into one of those comedies of manners the British are so good at. The comedy springs mainly from Ghote's ineptitude with the finer points of the English language and pronunciation. It is amazing that the English continue to derive so much profit from their former colonies, if not in raw materials like cotton and coal, certainly from the linguistic *faux pas* committed by Indians. It never occurs to the British, that if the tables were turned, if the British had to speak an Indian language (which they seldom bother to do), then *they* could expect to become the butts of social comedy. Here is an example of an unfair exchange. When Ghote meets Douglas Kerr, the British film star, the ensuing dialogue points up the fact that Ghote's ineptitude with English results in his constantly being corrected. Thus, Ghote, the Inspector of Police, becomes a schoolboy to the film star's lofty headmaster:

> "Is it you are pleased to be back once more in India, Mr. Douglas Kerr?"
> "Prefer to be called Carr, if you don't mind, old boy.

Pronounced Carr. Surprised you don't know that, if you're
as much a fan of my work as you said you were."

"Oh, yes, indeed, Mr. Douglas Kerr—Mr. Carr. I was
always a very, very great admirer of your many feats."

"Only two, old boy."

"Only two feats? But I am thinking—"

"Feet. Feet, old boy. Things you have on the end of
your legs, don't you know."

In a moment or little longer, Ghote had got the joke.
He laughed. (7-8)

Any authority that Ghote might possess is constantly
undermined by Kerr's school-masterish attitude. If the
situation was reversed and an Indian film star
encountered a British cop in London, the latter's total
ignorance of the former's language would not become a
matter for comedy. Then the Indian's lack of English
would be a handicap. In other words, the British not only
impose their language on their colonies but use that very
language to deepen their own sense of superiority.

Laboring as he does from a bottomless sense of
inadequacy, Ghote further complicates his life by taking on
the added burden of protecting naive foreigners. Besides
having to look after an aging, possibly alcoholic British
star, Ghote finds himself bustling an American sociologist
who is doing a study of the "behavioral attitudes among
third world prostitutes" into the safety of a taxi, after
advising her to find an Indian sociologist to accompany
her into this unsavory area. This little encounter, and
Ghote's advice, is not extraneous to the plot; it is an
integral part of the tapestry of crime and detection that
Keating weaves so skillfully, although it seems as artless
and uncontrived as the fabric of everyday life.

Giving considerable thought to keeping Kerr from
getting into trouble, Ghote decides that he needs the help
of Dr. Framrose, Sexologist, F.R.C.S. (U.K.), *Sex Diseases,
Sex Changes*, as the painted sign on the wall of his clinic

proclaims. Perhaps the doctor could more effectively warn Kerr about the dangers of diseases rampant in the area. The doctor's very first words are enough to chill the ardor of the doughtiest: "...come to see the coupling and copulating going full swing. You know what it all means to me? I'll tell you. Buboes and itches, sores and syphilis. That's what it all amounts to in the end, see it from my point of view" (12). With this warning ringing in their ears, and accompanied by the doctor, they visit a house, run by a typical gharwali, a madam "as rapacious, unfeeling and self-seeking a woman as you could find..."(12).

Just as the three of them climb the stairs to Heera's establishment on the fourth floor, Ghote is almost shocked into immobility—the handsome profile hurrying away furtively through the far corner, accompanied by a fat figure of the gharwali belongs to none other than the famous Sheriff of Bombay, a prestigious post, largely ceremonial, held by India's best loved cricketer and member of a royal family, Randhir Singh, the Rajah of Dar. Ghote's acute disillusionment at seeing his hero in such sordid surroundings turns into intense dismay when, alerted by the obvious distress of a young prostitute at what she sees behind a closed door, Ghote finds the horribly beaten and strangled body of another prostitute. Ghote has no doubt at all as to who has committed the horrible crime. It must be the Rajah of Dar who was being so obviously hurried away by the madam. The question is, how can Ghote prove it? Even though he instantly commandeers the whip used to flog the victim, how could he possibly get the sheriff's fingerprints without accusing him? How could he even get the ACP to entertain the thought that such a well loved national hero as Randy, as he is familiarly known, could have committed such a heinous crime?

What follows after this unpromising, or rather all too promising, start is one of Keating's most complex novels.

Notice I did not say a mystery or detective novel. It is not a detective or mystery novel in the conventional sense, in that it does not follow the pattern of murder—investigation—solution. Here the murderer is well known; indeed Ghote manages to get a set of fingerprints from the Sheriff on the pretext of getting a photograph of the famous cricketer signed for his son and the fingerprints exactly match those on the whip found in the dead woman's room. But as the ACP points out, there is no witness to corroborate Ghote's word that the whip was actually taken from the victim's room. Ghote had sneaked it out for fear that the venal D'Silva who is actually in charge of the case might be bribed into losing it. Even when Ghote points out that the murderer, so obviously a maniac, is a danger to the public, the ACP makes light of the fact: "To the public, Ghote? Well, you can call it the public if you like. But the fellow, even if he wasn't some local *dada* taking revenge on a girl who had stepped out of line, is obviously going to confine his activities to the prostitute class. I don't think it's a matter that need worry us at headquarters. Dismiss, Inspector" (30). In other words, justice is graded, as always, according to class.

But Ghote's grim determination to make an airtight case that will stick against his eminence, the Sheriff, leads him into an exploration of the world of prostitution and on a philosophical level, of the theme of the deceptiveness of appearances. The non-mystery that Ghote solves turns out to be the deeper mystery of life's unpredictable complexities.

Keating does not fall into the trap of portraying all prostitutes as miserable victims of society. Most of them are indeed victims, forced into the profession by their circumstances, but some of them manage to enjoy themselves. As a young prostitute tells Ghote about the woman who was murdered:

"She was a kolaki girl," Munni answered. "You know in that community when they are old enough they have to choose: will they have a husband or will they go in for prostitution line? And Kamala—she told me often—had seen the *jogtis* walking happily, carrying shining images of gods and goddesses and shouting praises and laughing always, and she knew she wanted to be one of them."

"And when she—when she became one, did it seem as good to her then?"

"Oh, there are some bad days always, but it was better than she thought even. Better better. She liked and liked and liked." (29)

Lest this may seem too rosy a picture, Keating portrays another prostitute, a married woman, deeply in love with her husband, who has been kidnapped, and tortured into a life that she loathes so much that she is almost prepared to die trying to escape it. Ghote, compassionate as ever, nearly loses sight of a witness while he takes the time and trouble to help the woman escape the clutches of her *gharwali*.

At the other end of the spectrum are two college students who also work as high-priced call girls. One of them, intelligent but born into a poor family, uses prostitution as a way to come into contact with the world of glamour, wealth and power, something she hankers for but which, as a woman from the lower classes, she will never be able to achieve on her own. With slight variations in circumstances, she can be seen as an Indian Madame Bovary, and may also expect to come to a grisly end as does her friend, a child of wealthy, but neglectful parents who becomes the second victim of the sex murderer. When Ghote wonders about the connection, the victim's friend tells Ghote that Usha, the murdered call girl, had given up prostitution as she had "caught a disease."

Then there are the Indian counterparts of the Japanese Geisha—born to an ancient profession where pleasing the senses include the superb pleasures of dance and music. Ghote, fixated on the seemingly incontrovertible empirical evidence of the Sheriff's guilt, follows him to the Pavan Pool

> that curious group of dwellings set around an inner compound that was the traditional home of Bombay's courtesans…. The courtesans, though ready to form liaisons with men either for the length of a night or in a more permanent way, were before anything else singers and dancers, entertainers deriving from the legendary courtesans of places like Lucknow in the north, the easers of the hard hours of Mogul princes. Ghote, engaged as he is in watching the Sheriff closely, cannot help being transported by one of the dancer's beauty and grace.

> Ghote, who had not often heard singing of this quality, was rapidly lost in it. And lost, too, in the skirt-lifting swirl of the young dancer, her whole body echoing the music as the drummer heightened his rhythm to an electric burst of sound. He felt as if he was being made love to, himself. And he was sure that the pot-bellied man in the corner felt just the same, as surely did the Sheriff, sitting entranced, his head very slightly moving to the music's beat. (144, 149-50)

Ghote's wanderings through the venal underworld of Bombay resembles Stephen Daedalus' nighttime quest in Joyce's *Ulysses*. Ghote receives an education not only in the varieties of sexual gratification available for money, the differing temperaments among the prostitutes, from Laxmi who hates her trade, to the rebellious Putla, to plump Munni "unable to understand how it could be unpleasant to make 'fun' with a whole beguiling variety of men" or the dead Kamala, the Kolati who had "chosen with open eyes the life of a prostitute and who had enjoyed it too" (168), but much more important, he gains an insight into the nature of imaginative transformation. "Yet, again, that depended on the way you looked. You could look at a courtesan in the book written hundreds of years ago as a figure of crystal. Or you could look on her as being just such another creature to be paid for as... As poor dead Kamala" (167).

As a result of his odyssey through the shoals of human desire, Ghote learns not only that appearances are deceptive, that the reality beneath is often startlingly different and more complex than the sum of empirical evidence that make up our sense impressions, but also that active, empathic imaginative energy and insight is needed to grasp the underlying tragic dignity of each human being, however pathetic or sordid on the outside. Thus, when Ghote's haste is impeded by a "cripple, one-legged and poling himself about with the aid of a long staff," Ghote's automatic response is to wonder, "What was a man like that doing here? Then, the answer came to him. He was doing just what all the other gapers and idlers were doing. Taking his pick. See him not as a cripple but as a man, and he was a man, a man with the same needs and desires as other men" (169).

Ghote's sudden illumination about the true identity of the murderer, an illumination that cuts across the invincible chain of logic and evidence that has shackled him till now, springs from an almost Shakespearean insight, the kind of insight born of understanding the nature of "topsy-turvy," the nature of carnival. According to the Russian critic Bakhtin, the anarchy implicit in the topsy turvy of carnival "creates" a truth far more true than the rigid categorizations of the work-a-day world of work. Thus appearance and reality are not opposites as much as equally true and co-existent. Ghote thinks about the college students/call girls, Usha and Sweetie:

Usha Wabgaonkar had been just such another example, too. Wanting respect, wanting a dignified life of a sort, wanting not to be a girl in some office looked down upon, rebuked and snubbed. And choosing to earn respect by losing it, or so to most people it would seem. By losing it as much as it possibly could be lost.

But other eyes, other views. And Usha and Sweetie Baskar had, for their different reasons, embraced the call-girl life while seeming to be no more than innocent students, girlish and giggling. While actually still being such gigglers. (170)

Ghote, an Indian policeman struggling with a language that by its very history masters him and reduces him to the position of a colonial subject manages, by the sheer power of empathic intelligence, to rise above his ingrained sense of inadequacy and grasp the infinite complexity of human beings. An insight expressed pithily by Shakespeare in *Twelfth Night*: "One face, one voice, one habit and two persons / A natural perspective, that is and is not!" (5.1.215-216).

When Ghote solves the murder, it is the result of this inspired, imaginative leap of a natural perspective in which the Sheriff, the glamorous cricketer and the dashing rake, turns out to be an oddly vulnerable human being. On the other hand, a healer turns out to be a destroyer in his very zeal to cleanse the world of physical and moral sickness. The trivial and the great, a trick picture, a word that Ghote does not know, but which he gnaws on till the meaning hits him with its deadly significance, all from a wonderful carnival of clues, even as Ghote participates in the carnival of desires in Bombay. The last lines, when the Sheriff does not recognize Ghote in his uniform, while Ghote is dreading the possibility of recognition, is the last little piece of comedy that falls neatly into the gigantic jigsaw puzzle that is and is not life. In *The Sheriff of Bombay* Keating pulls off the ultimate coup—a novel that is and is not both an unpretentious mystery and a profound novel that explores the mystery of life itself.

The traditional mystery form is blithely abandoned in *Under A Monsoon Cloud*. It is as if Keating had said to himself: To hell with the whodunit format—discovery of the body, questioning of suspects; dovetailing of alibis and motive, unmasking of the culprit; I want to examine a moral issue unfettered by the classic form. So instead of a mystery, we have a suspense novel, instead of a murder, we have a culpable homicide. The formidable Additional Deputy Inspector-General of Police, Kelkar, famous for his temper and his integrity, hurls a brass inkpot at a bumbling fool of a Sergeant and kills him, watched by a horrified Ghote and the reader. Events, however, take a bizarre turn when Ghote who had long hero-worshipped Kelkar, refuses to arrest him even when ordered to do so by Kelkar himself. Instead, to his own astonishment and the reader's dismay, Ghote persuades Kelkar to conceal the body and all the evidence of murder.

The premise that our hero, Ghote, who however diffident, however comic, is always so scrupulously honest, could go to the lengths of concealing a homicide because of his admiration for the culprit strains our credibility. Nothing in the portrayal of Ghote thus far leads to this implausible deviation of character and behavior. Ghote has been built up as the consummate policeman, forever recalling the precise words of Hans Gross' *Criminal Investigation*, his secular bible. If anything, Ghote's problem is that he sticks to police procedure in all its dullest, most routine aspects, without resorting to the usual short cuts—torturing a confession out of a suspect, for example which his more venal colleagues are prone to do. Even all his personal relationships including his elegant, spirited wife and adored son, are sidelined by his devotion to duty. That such a man would collude with his boss, however admired, to conceal the killing of a hapless underling strains belief.

What makes the plot barely credible is that Ghote is led to his highly uncharacteristic action by his admiration for Kelkar's least admirable trait—his temper: "Yes, Tiger and his searching, saving anger had to be preserved, cost what it might" (28). Cost what it might? When it means the life of a human being, however ineffectual, as the Sergeant undoubtedly was? This seems an extraordinary argument, even for someone blinded by hero-worship. Surely, efficiency can be achieved without the kind of anger, born of self-righteous arrogance, as Kelkar's seems to be. For guilty as he is, indebted to Ghote as he becomes, Kelkar continues to bully Ghote as he was wont to do: there is not a hint of humility or self-reproach in his subsequent behavior. That Ghote should in his own words, be "more committed to Tiger, to anger-fuelled Tiger, than he was to the code of police conduct which he thought had entered into his very bones" (28), boggles the imagination. If a willing suspension of disbelief is the sine-quo-non of detective fiction, with its roots in the social realities of crime and punishment, then *Under A Monsoon Cloud* does not quite make it. The very moral premise of the novel, so given to exploring moral questions, is bizarrely skewed.

However, the novel does manage to retain a grip, albeit shaky, on the reader, because of Keating's evocation of a teeming Bombay battered by an unusually severe monsoon. The effects of relentless rain on the overcrowded, less than efficient, cosmopolitan city, and especially on the thousands of homeless pavement dwellers is portrayed vividly. Besides the literal description of the rain and its effects on daily life, the rain also provides a self-aggrandizing metaphor for Ghote's own inexplicable shielding of a murderer:

> He had seen himself as God Krishna, no less, blue-bodied and beautiful of limb as in the calendar pictures, holding aloft, umbrella-like, Steep Mount Godharvan so as to protect from the fury of the terrible storm above, not all the people of the village of Braj but simply Tiger, a harassed and momentarily anger-deprived Tiger. (47-48)

Keating ties in the Hindu myth beautifully with other details of plot, locale and atmosphere. The town to which Ghote had been temporarily posted, and in which Kelkar had killed the Sergeant during a tour of inspection, is named Vigatpore, the Town of Difficulties. It has a modest reputation as a hill station because of its temperate climate and the beautiful Lake Helena which dominates it, but during Ghote's stay in it, everything that could possibly go wrong does go wrong, thus making the name eponymous.

Then there is the portrayal of a host of entirely believable characters. Kelkar, unable to live with himself, commits suicide without implicating Ghote's role in his actions. However, when an inquiry is instituted, the suspense picks up in a way reminiscent of the courtroom scenes in a Perry Mason novel. There is a variegated array of types, from the westernized lawyer for the prosecution to the Marxist-feminist lawyer, Mrs. Ahmed, who true to her principles, works for the People's Union for Civil Liberties and is a Hindu married to a Moslem, thus earning social, including Ghote's own, disapprobation. However, Ghote decides that Mrs. Ahmed's social conscience and anger would be most useful in salvaging his own seemingly hopeless case. Then there are the illiterate and seemingly gullible villagers who manage to hold their own during the forbidding legal proceedings. Finally, there is the temple priest Ghote reluctantly goes to for advice (more to appease his wife than because he believes in religious solace), who in suitably enigmatic words counsels Ghote to carry on the good fight and not give up.

Unlike most Western and westernized (Naipaul, for example) novelists who portray the extremes of sophistication and traditionalism, Keating conveys its intricate blend that is India. When Ghote does go to the temple, it is not because, as Naipaul would say, westernization is a veneer and Hindu superstition the bedrock reality, but because in the give and take of a close marriage, such as Ghote's and Protima's, one does compromise one's innate skepticism in the interests of domestic peace. Besides, Ghote benefits from going along with his wife because he realizes that such binary oppositions as rational/irrational do not do justice to the complexity of daily life. It is this densely textured feel for life in India which finally makes the novel worthwhile in spite of its initial implausibilities. The very slow pace of the first few chapters, like the slow wearing away of the spirit by the incessant rain, finally envelops the reader in a dense, damp miasma of contradictions that is Indian life.

Ghote's moral dilemma—to persist in a lie or not—is resolved when he finally realizes that Kelkar's anger is not the best or the only way to achieve desired results. During the painstakingly slow proceedings of the legal inquiry, Ghote observes and has time to reflect on another police officer, the very image of serenity, the very opposite of Kelkar, who had been just as efficient and honest. The saying, "Lords without anger or honour, who dare not carry their sword always" had always come to his mind whenever he had to justify Kelkar at work. But he realizes that "Nadkarni ever quiet, ever calm had carried [also] his sword always" (184).

He further asks himself:

> Would old Nadkarni have been as sharply furious with one and all as Tiger if he had been sent in his day as in-charge at Vigatpore?
>
> No. No, he would not have been, of course. He would have confronted each offender with his fault, have pointed it out to him, exactly, quietly. And, by the very steadiness he showed, he would have brought about reform.... Perhaps the inkpot would never have got spilt, if the whole business had been conducted quietly yet forcefully. And then the inkpot would not have been hurled in rage and Desai at this moment would be alive and well and hopelessly foolish.

Yes, Tiger's anger had often achieved results, better
results than he himself would have got, but it had its other
side too. When Tiger had thrown that inkpot it had not been
out of any cleansing rage. It had been out of uncontrolled,
dangerous anger. Just that. (205-206)

This blinding insight into the essentially useless and
destructive nature of anger helps Ghote to regain his
moral equilibrium. His brief deviation from his true self is
over as he makes the right moral choice at the risk of
losing his cherished career as a policeman. However, S.M.
Motabhoy, the presiding officer, after pronouncing a
verdict of guilty and pronouncing the maximum
punishment, inexplicably omits to fulfill a small, but
crucial legal obligation, thus nullifying the verdict. The
novel ends with the official end of the monsoon, marked
by the celebration of *NARELI PURNIMA*, Coconut Day. At
Chaupatti Beach, Ghote, his wife Protima and son Ved
join the immense throng collected there to immerse
coconuts. As Ved displays a flash of temper at some
urchins who nab his coconut, Protima rebukes Ghote for
not getting angry at the boys. Ghote's reply sums up the
change in his thinking: "No," he said, "it is best for me to
keep my anger until a time when it will be truly needed"
(22).

Keating's love of spoofing the conventions of detective
fiction reaches its comic apotheosis in *The Body in the
Billiard Room*. As the title indicates, the novel is ostensibly
in the tradition of the golden age of mystery fiction,
suggesting neatly murdered bodies behind closed doors in
an upper-class sporty setting, much given to displays of
hunting, fishing and snooker trophies. Ghote is sent by
his boss to the very British hill resort of Ootacomond in
South India where the relics of the British empire huddle
together in an exclusive club, warming themselves at the
embers of rituals left over from the hey day of the British
raj.

When Ghote arrives in Ooty after a long, carefully described bus journey through the winding hills, he realizes he has come to a fairy tale world which could be either, in his words, "paradise Ooty, hell Ooty" (24). It feels like paradise because the cool air of the hill station reminds him that he has escaped the "heat of the turbid plains" into a magical world which seems ye olde world British, full of neat little tiled cottages covered with climbing roses named Glen view, Harrow-on-the-Hill, Woodbriar, Stella Cottage, Dahlia Bank, Clifton Villa and so on, with all its attendant sense of law and order which the British like to think they are the very source and fount. At the station, he is met by a former Ambassador, His Excellency Surinder Mehta, who had asked for Ghote's services on the strength of the praises sung about him by that "fool of a British writer" (10) who had once watched him at work. This sly reference to Keating occurs again later on in the novel when one of Keating's own mysteries, published under the pseudonym, Evelyn Hervey, becomes instrumental in providing Ghote with an important clue.

This self-referential spoofing of mystery fiction provides the deep structure of the novel, the rigid spine of which is His Excellency, Surinder Mehta, an ardent fan of the genre who can not only quote chapter and verse from the golden-age of detective fiction, but constantly confuses the reality of murder with the fantasies of crime spun by mystery writers. Ghote, whose knowledge of detective fiction is sketchy at best, is forced into a role which, given his innate realism and modesty, makes him very uncomfortable—the role alternately of Sherlock Holmes or Hercule Poirot, with the former Ambassador as his Dr. Watson or Inspector Lestrade. In the topsy turvy world of Ooty where fiction and reality change places constantly, the roles of detective and sidekick are also reversed, with Mr. Mehta in his role of Watson directing the precise moves to be made by his superior, Holmes.

Ghote's sense of unreality is further heightened when he is informed that nothing is to be gained by the normal police procedures of searching the murder site for clues. The body of Picchu, the billiards marker, had been found the day before, carefully laid out on the billiard table, with only a neat little stab wound indicating that he was not merely in an alcohol-induced sleep. To Ghote's consternation, he learns that the local Inspector has not only summarily removed the body, careless of any clues, but in addition, had not ordered a post-mortem and had declared that the murder was committed during a robbery, or in Indian parlance, a decoity, of the silver sporting trophies which it was part of Picchu's duties to guard. But Mr. Mehta insists that it could not have been a run-of-the-mill robbery because of the orderliness with which the murder was committed and the body disposed on the table. Playing his self-appointed role as the Great Detective's stooge, Mehta has found out that Picchu was a nasty piece of goods and, judging from his luxurious possessions, a blackmailer as well. So he is determined that the murder should conform exactly to the pattern used over and over again by Dame Agatha Christie: "Yes. Just like in the books. The circumstances that make it clear that only a limited number of suspects could have committed the crime.... The situation here is precisely that of a Christie story" (22-23). Mr. Mehta also insists on seeing the club as a snowbound manor house as in Christie's *Sittaford Mystery* and the members as the seven suspects in Michael Innes' novel of the same name.

Ghote tries to retain his sanity in this inspired craziness by stubbornly clinging to the humdrum police procedures of interviewing the suspects and applying logic to what turns out to be a tangled web of irrational, thoroughly human, unpredictable behavior of the club members. *The Body in the Billiards Room* makes no pretense to being a fully-fleshed, realistic novel. Its characters are not merely stereotypes; rather, they are broadly drawn caricatures, milked for all their comic potential. There is the Maharajah of Pratapgadh who insists on making Ghote his golfing partner, and who cheats blatantly, counting on Ghote's ignorance of the rules of the game. His luscious but bitchy wife, the Maharani, carries on an affair with an indigent student in a sordid hotel and is righteously indignant when she learns about her husband's liaison with a well-known film star. There is the corpulent Moslem Habidulla, who eats only dessert—roly poly pudding—and nothing else. There is Miss Lucy Trayling who thinks of England as home but stays on to nurse her ailing ayah, exhibiting the self-proclaimed British traits of loyalty and courage in the face of adversity. Then there is Major Bell who has won a coveted award for his prowess in snooker who lives alone with his decrepit dog in a decrepit house. Then there is Mr. Iyer, the secretary who recalls P.G. Wodehouse's fictional character, the efficient Baxter. Finally, there is the Professor of English literature, named, tongue in cheek, Godbole, after the character in E.M. Forster's *A Passage to India* who discourses learnedly on the archetypal nature of the Great Detective: "Holmes is a person, a super-person one might say, of a unique sort. He is a man able to combine at the highest level the intuitive powers of the poet with the powers of logical analysis of the mathematician" (77).

It is Godbole, professor and high priest, who educates the empirical, logical policeman, Ghote, to entertain the heady freedom of poetic insights. Ghote, stubbornly resistant to intuitive flights thanks to his British police training, admits defeat after deductive analysis of all the tortuous trails of shameful secrets and blackmail and other evidence fails to solve the identity of the murderer. On the verge of giving up and returning to crowded, chaotic, but very real Bombay, Ghote is persuaded to attend a lecture on the Great Detective by Godbole. Ghote finds himself listening to his words with fascinated concentration:

"We are, are we not," the little brahmin said, favouring his scattered audience with a sharply wicked grin, "each one of us trapped? Trapped within our own personalities. Over the years we build up in our minds a picture of ourselves. A picture of a person we can bear to live with, perhaps often a person of whom we are secretly proud...but a picture that we create for ourselves in this way has a most terrible effect. It places round us limits. It lays down for us rules, rules we dare not break even though they are rules we alone have devised. But the Great Detective...Ah the Great Detective, he—or sometimes she—in the pages of those books we delight to read, can by the force of genius show us these rules being broken. He shows us that the prisons we make for ourselves can be escaped from...

Yes, the Great Detectives, whilst we read with simple pleasure of the triumphs, can teach us by the secret ways of imaginative writing that it is possible to escape from the prisons, the locked rooms, imposed on us by our own egos. Now, what is one of the ways, perhaps the most striking in which this lesson is presented to us? Why, by the simple, and always intriguing device of disguise. In that notable tale *A Scandal in Bohemia* we read of Mr. Sherlock Holmes disguising himself as a drunken groom, making himself—note—wholly into a person smelling equally of the horse and the bottle. And we realize then, without realizing that we have realized it, that other people exist....He has to recognize, for himself and for us also, that the whole outside world is there. A world beyond him, a world of the other." (196-197).

Godbole's speech has a galvanizing effect on Ghote's spirits. He sets out to put himself in the proper meditative frame of mind suitable for sparking the intuitive leap which transcends the built-in limitations of logic. To do this he has a choice of two techniques—Indian and Western. Indian by birth and upbringing but Western by virtue of his police training, Ghote can choose either the

Hindu discipline of yoga or some of the techniques of Sherlock Holmes: both are aids to achieving a trance-like state of mind conducive to free association.

There are comic descriptions of Ghote sitting in the lotus position and concentrating on the tip of his nose—as recommended by Dr. Joshi in his book on yoga. Having failed to achieve *dharana* or yogic trance, Ghote decides to try the "Great Detective way"—smoking a pipe a la Sherlock Holmes. Ghote buys a cheap pipe and tobacco (because Spencer's Stores is "Sunday-closed") from a street vendor and doggedly puffs away as he strolls around Ooty wondering, "Should he try combining pipe yoga with Dr. Joshi's? Concentrating perhaps, not on the tip of his nose, but on the smoke-curling bowl of his pipe?" (229). Nothing happens except that after leaving the town, he wanders into more rugged country where "wooded ravines," and a "silver stream" put him in mind of wild beasts. A combination of cheap tobacco and rarefied mountain air makes him feel giddy and nauseous. Pausing to rest on a rock, throwing away the pipe in disgust, he again savors bitter defeat. Finally, wandering back to the town, his mind empty of thought, he hears the chimes of St. Stephen's Church. Standing still in appreciation, he realizes that he has experienced the "Great Detective's trance" and the knowledge of who it was who had been Picchu's poisoner had flowered in his mind. Everything had mysteriously come together at the very back of his head, in the innermost recesses" (229).

Ghote lays his chain of largely circumstantial evidence before the Ambassador and because he has no actual proof that would hold up in a court of law, decides to confront the murderer and extract a confession. In true implausible British mystery fiction manner, the murderer, a true Brit to the last, acknowledges his guilt and obligingly shoots himself. A dignified exit in British upper-class tradition immortalized by Shakespeare in his description of the traitor Thane of Cawdor's conduct during his execution.

"Nothing in his life became him like the leaving of it" (*Macbeth* i. iv. 7-8). Such dignity in death is not allowed the lower orders of course, as they are summarily taken off to be tried and hanged.

In real life there are several less noble, more plausible solutions to upper-class crime: first, it is very seldom that a crime is brought home to a member of the ruling class and second, even if it is, his peers ensure that it is covered up so that the dignity of the individual and by extension, of the whole class, is preserved intact. They have the education and writing skills to construct an elaborate mythology which ensures not only the maintenance of their status-quo but the very self-aggrandizing myths which help them to stay in power and exploit the masses. However, to apply the constraints of painful social realities to such a frothy concoction as *The Body in the Billiard Room*, is to paraphrase the Bard, taste with a distempered appetite and mistake bird bolts for cannon bullets. Indeed, in Keating's hands, the rigid format of the classic detective novel becomes capable of yielding extraordinary flights of fancy and imagination which ironically yield greater, if fitful illuminations into that dark, often impenetrable interstices of life.

Keating's latest novel to date, *Dead on Time*, is one more fine example of his preoccupation with abstract philosophical issues as they are actually experienced by a variety of people—from the Director General of Maharashtra police to the beggar on the street. The novel begins with the former, a study in the comedy of power, tapping his brand new watch, a "new Tata Titon Quartz" named Exacto and commending poor Ghote for being "Dead on Time." The novel ends with Ghote arriving 21 minutes late to DGP's office to make his final report, dreading the consequences of his unpunctuality, only to find that his boss had forgotten to wear his Exacto and just assumes that Ghote is punctual. As Ghote tells one of his rare lies, that he is indeed on time, he reflects "I am dead on time, after all. In a way" (202). The nature of time, the way different cultures, Western and Eastern, conceive of it, and its tragic consequences in the lives of people, forms the core of Ike novel.

The murder victim is well connected—he is the grandson and sole heir of a powerful village headman Pendke, who commands 10,000 votes in the local election. The DGP has been tipped off by a colleague in the village that the headman has another grandson, "a thoroughly bad hat," who stands to inherit from his grandfather now, and is perfectly capable of having done away with his paternal cousin. The DGP has already booked a ticket for Ghote on the train to Nagpur, the closest railway station to the village. It is immediately obvious to Ghote that he has been assigned the absurd, impossible task of looking into the affairs of a powerful village headman that no one wants to antagonize, and find a "solution" that does not rock the various political boats that are afloat on very murky waters.

Pressed for time, bound by the implacable demands of clocks and schedules, Ghote decides to make his inquiries at the scene of the crime and takes the train to Nagpur, the closest stop to the village. He does not learn much there, but almost misses the train when he is accosted by a madman, who queries insistently, "Time Kya?" It turns out that the madman had been a timekeeper for the local bus stop before misfortune befell him. Ghote notes, but fails to understand, the significance of the long scar beneath the man's rib cage and the murder victim's recent medical history—he was recovering from a kidney transplant operation when he was killed. After a series of mishaps that make nonsense of Ghote's efforts to be punctual, he reaches the village Rhamked. He realizes immediately that here, "Time would not be measured even in days and weeks, but in the slow sound of the six seasons, spring into the hot weather, hot weather into the rains, rains into autumn, autumn into winter, winter into the cold weather, cold weather into spring once more" (24).

This central theme of the relative nature of time is voiced cogently by the village headman whose gargantuan figure alone is enough to inspire awe. When Ghote tries to explain that it is crucial to establish the exact time the murder was committed as well as the whereabouts of the principal suspect, the village headman erupts with the following piece of phenomenology:

> Times, times...Do not be talking to me about your times for this and times for that. That is what you city people are not understanding. What does it matter whether it is one minute more, or five minutes less? I will tell you what is mattering, Mr. Police. It is not how you can eat up time, gobble, gobble, gobble, as fast as you can because you are fearful there is not enough of it. It is letting time go through yourself. It is being there and knowing and feeling it, that is what you should be doing with time. (60)

This ability to know and feel every moment of life deeply is exactly what is lacking in Sub Inspector Lobo, for instance, whose shallowness, as opposed to the headman's depth and wisdom, is what leads to the false arrest, torture and forced confession of the supposed murderer, the hapless Rustom. "Speedy" Lobo made that "false jump in logic" precisely because he never paused to reflect, to experience and to savor life. Ghote who is a police officer in "hurry-scurry" Bombay can neither afford to follow the leisurely path advocated by the headman, nor does he approve of the over hasty expeditiousness of Inspector Lobo.

Having experienced both city time and village timelessness, Ghote is ultimately led, as always, by a leap of insight to the solution of the crime, but not till Ghote experiences village life in all its varied aspects. Keating captures the crazy-quilt of rural India without the sardonic condescension of a Naipaul or the bitter misanthropism of a Jhabvala. Just as in the city, the village of Rhamked has its usual mix of fools, saints and villains. There are lovely portraits of a young Bhrahmin priest, who is what he professes to be; there is an aged mother who unquestioningly offers Ghote, who has come to question her son, her unstinting hospitality. Ghote savors the moments of utter tranquility which take him back to his own uncomplicated childhood:

> So he wandered onward, easily and amiably, as the cows coming in twos and threes toward him with a small boy or two armed with frail pieces of stick occasionally remembering to urge them on.
>
> How different these animals are, he reflected, from the skinny-ribbed scavengers of the streets in Bombay, almost as sharply acquisitive as Bombayites themselves going about their grabbing, not-a-moment-to lose business. Here each flop eared animal seemed sleek and contented, calmly approaching the evening tryst with the milking pail. Swaying gently from side to side, sending up with each easy pace one more puff of dust to add to the floating cloud around and above. Tranquility grew in him with every step. The DGP's urgency fell into place in his mind. (67)

Such romanticizing of village life, however, is destined to be shattered. As he wanders on, the villain Ganpatrao, deliberately runs him down with his motor bike. Ghote's quick thinking saves him, but barely. He arrives in Bombay, bloody, bruised, and shaken. The solution to the crime lies in the urban bustle of Bombay where the rich business class and the destitute are linked by the medical profession which must serve both impartially, but which finds itself inevitably favoring the rich at the expense of the poor. It is in this cruel inequality, engendered by a Hobbesian society, that the roots of crime can be found.

The novel, tightly structured like an Agatha Christie mystery, shot through with satirical digs at the pomposity of bureaucrats, village headmen et al., portrays an interesting array of characters who manage to retain their individuality and humanity against overwhelming odds. The theme of different conceptions of time, their relative merits and demerits is treated with a light touch in keeping with the essentially playful puzzle form of the whodunit. Altogether an enjoyable book spiked with some serious reflections and observations.

The latest Keating novel to date, *The Iciest Sin*, bears an epigraph by Rebecca West: "Blackmail is the Iciest Sin." Blackmail, from the childish (little Ved, Ghote's only son tries to blackmail his father into buying him a home computer) to the truly evil is the leit motif of Keating's novel. Ghote is sent by Z.R. Mistry, Additional Secretary in the Department of Home, to entrap "the most dangerous woman in Bombay," a Miss Dolly Daruwala who has his cousin, a tax consultant, in her clutches. She has managed to steal from his office a document which conclusively proves that he has helped his clients engage in tax fraud.

Keating seems to have written this novel as a tribute to the Parsee community in India. The Parsees, known for their distinctive religion (Zoroastrianism, with roots in Persia) and culture, are also noted for their entrepreneurial success and their philanthropy. As usual, Keating gets all the cultural minutiae exactly right, but alas, the plot gets so implausible that it strains the willing suspension of disbelief necessary for the reader to keep reading. What stretches our credulity to the breaking point is that Ghote, who for all his comic absurdity earns the reader's respect by stubbornly clinging to his professional integrity, does something at the very beginning of the book that violates the most sacred of police codes: he witnesses a murder and chooses not only to let the murderer escape, but actually helps him to cover up his tracks. He willingly and consciously decides to become an accessory after the fact, because the murderer is a well-known and respected scientist whose latest project will be of great benefit to the poor. Ghote's complicity in the crime comes about when he is asked to break into Daruwala's apartment and witness her attempt to blackmail and then to arrest the woman on the spot.

That a Bombay police officer breaks into an apartment under official orders is bad enough, but having arrived there, Ghote, hidden under the bed, witnesses Dr. Edul Commissariat, the scientist, stab his blackmailer with a knife concealed in his walking stick. It turns out that Daruwala had in her possession the scientist's thesis, distinctly inferior to the one he had stolen from his dying cousin and had passed off as his own. Astoundingly, Ghote not only lets him get away with it but works to protect him from discovery! He rationalizes his unpoliceman-like conduct this way:

> He had rapidly come to feel, to believe absolutely that the Parsi scientist was right to have made away with Dolly Daruwala. She had been calmly proposing to prevent him using this superconductor of his to pull the mass of his fellow countrymen out of the desperate poverty in which so many of them seemed to be sucked. That alone, set aside all the other victims icily tortured over the years, was sufficient reason if ever there was reason enough to condemn him. (31)

From this very uncharacteristic, unbelievable twist in logic and Ghote's character, as he has been presented until now (with the exception of *Under a Monsoon Cloud*, perhaps a foreshadowing of Ghote's downward slide on the moral scale?), compounded by the fact that the murder was coldly premeditated—Dr. Commissariat had brought a swordstick—other implausible actions follow. Ghote is seen leaving the flat and is soon blackmailed by Mistry's peon and later, a notorious druglord blackmails Ghote into becoming an informant about the drug raids the police are about to launch. This chain of collusion in crime by Ghote inevitably leads to the climax when Ghote decides to murder the druglord by pushing him under a speeding train. Just when the reader is about to give up on Ghote and his creator, Ghote is brought to his senses by his inability to commit a murder. Phew! Saved at the brink! The novel leaves one with the uncomfortable sensation of a contrived resolution to the plot without the necessary cathartic relief. Dr. Commissariat, one presumes, is walking around the earth, an arrogant scientist, making decisions of life and death like a petty god, with the full knowledge and approval of Ghote. Keating presents the insulated world of the Parsees exactly right, in keeping with his unerring eye for distinctive social groups, but somewhere along the way, he sends Ghote into a novelistic limbo, with a moral vision skewed beyond a reader's forgiveness.

The Non-Ghote Fiction

Keating embarked on his career as a prolific writer of mysteries with the publication of *Death and the Visiting Firemen*. Keating has said that "...in writing fiction, as well as in my manner of looking at life as it trundles by, the distant view is my way" (Autobiography Series Vol. 8 163), but in his very first novel, he chooses a setting that he knew intimately. He had taken a coach tour from Bath to London as a reporter for the *Wiltshire Herald* in 1953, to convey "loyal greetings" for the coronation of Queen Elizabeth and he decided to utilize his experience for the novel.

Death and the Visiting Firemen deals with a group of English actors and actresses who entertain a delegation from the American Institution for the Investigation of Incendiarism, Inc., by dressing up in Victorian costumes and travelling with them in a coach across England. The trip includes a mock holdup which provides the right opportunity for the murder—the highwayman is shot by one of the passengers. The ensuing scenario is in the tradition of the classic British mystery: it has a limited number of eccentric suspects holed up at various country inns. The Dickensian cast of characters includes a Latin-quoting schoolmaster and his sidekick, a young scapegrace reminiscent of the members of Holmes'

Baker Street gang. There are also some romantic goings on between mannered young women and their equally artificial young men.

On the jacket, a blurb by the noted crime critic Julian Symons praises Keating because he "Blends a quirky humor of scene and epithet with a delicious formal irony in the handling of dialogue." However, I found both the humor and the dialogue labored and tedious, particularly the reflexive tic of authorial comment on the characters' dialogue as if Keating cannot bring himself to trust the reader's comprehension. Here is a sample:

> The girl floundered round.
> "Richard."
> Her voice a coo, but importunate.
> "Yes?"
> The actor acknowledged no debt.
> No overt debt. (3)

The characters are already well enough established to be utterly predictable in their responses and the author's commentary merely lengthens out what is already an overlong book. Far from being a felicitous mix, the blending of knock-down drag-out farce, stilted dialogue, cardboard characters and a barely convincing mystery makes the novel a beginning writer's uneasy attempt to find himself a place in a heavily populated genre. It is only later when he looked to an utterly alien country like India and decided to stand the genre on its head that Keating truly came into his own as an original mystery writer.

Zen There was Murder anticipates, in a rudimentary way, Keating's later penchant for using the mystery form for the exploration of philosophical issues, particularly the major theme in most of his Ghote novels—the limitations of logical thinking and the possibilities of intuitive modes of knowing. The novel also anticipates Keating's fascination with Eastern philosophy. In this novel, as the title indicates, Zen provides the means of discovering whodunit. The setting for the crime, committed with the ceremonial knife used in Japan to commit harakiri, is a country mansion converted to adult educational courses. Mr. Utamuro, described in stereotypical ways, given to gnomic utterances such as, "The moon shines on the water, the water reflects the moon. What exactly is there? The—moon—in—the water. Without the moon it is not, without the water it is not. Together it is the moon in the water" (68) is the Master who teaches a course on Zen, who also solves the murder. At the very beginning of the novel, Utamuro's basic premise is established as antithetical to cherished Western values: "Intelligence is a great trap. It makes us look for what we think aught to be there, not what we would see if only we looked without thinking" (72).

The students in his course, also the suspects in the subsequent murder of a fellow student, are not up to the philosophical weight of Mr. Utamuro's sophistries. Drawn extremely sketchily, they hark back to the stock types of British Edwardian drawing room comedies: the philandering twit, the dim clergyman, the jealous wife, the stolid matron, the flirtatious red-head and a pair of au-pair girls with the requisite heavy accents. The dialogue is equally leaden, with the novelist underscoring the nuances of every exchange with a heavy hand, making the reader feel that she is somehow not up to "getting" all the (un)subtleties.

The following exchange between the Superintendent of Police and Mr. Utamuro is instructive in the embarrassing oversimplifications that result in the uncomprehending clash of cultures:

> "Yes, sir, you have. I make no bones about it. Flagrantly to suggest that you will conceal information: it may be well enough in Japan—I don't know how the police conduct themselves there—but let me make it clear here and now, it won't do in England."
>
> Mr. Utamuro grinned again.
>
> "I am afraid I intended to upset you," he said.
>
> "You intended to upset me?"
>
> Incredulity.
>
> "Yes, I wanted to make you understand from the start. It is what you would call fair that you should know. You see, superintendent, I have trained my mind to the point where such things as the idea of justice, the notion of a citizen's duty, the concept of illegality, all mean nothing to me. If you understand that, you will know where you are. And that is important."
>
> "We'll get this straight," said the superintendent. His eyes fixed on Mr. Utamuro. "You are telling me that in certain circumstances you would do all you could to prevent me arresting a murderer?"
>
> "No, I am not saying that though it might prove to be true. You see, even logic means nothing to me.'
>
> "Stop."
>
> The superintendent held up his right hand.
>
> "Now listen," he said, "I don't happen to have had any experience of the Far East, but naturally I've

read about your mysteries and the sort of things they do. All right, all that is beyond me, but I suppose it means a lot to you. But, understand this much, when you're over here it won't wash. You'll have to drop it. You'll have to go by the rules of plain ordinary common sense for a bit." (134)

As is usual in classic British mysteries, the rules of plain, ordinary common sense hobble the police in a way that the flights of Utamuro's intuition do not, and he finally lays bare the motivations of the murderer, who is, also in keeping with tradition, the least likely suspect. The motivation does not reside, as literary critics would like to have it, in the sociology of crime but in domestic passions gone awry. Mr. Utamuro, for all his philosophical abstractions, is keenly empirical in his approach to life and deduction. He solves the puzzle by paying close, unbiased attention to every minute detail of speech and behavior. As he says to the suspects, "Bet the man who has abandoned reason is the one to see through false reasoning" (217). The incomprehension of the West is nowhere better illustrated than in the clergyman's final comment, "Such a pity that it is only one of the fancier products of the human mind. Such a pity that its main effect is to cut us off from the truth" (217). This comment is the acme of unintended irony, considering that Mr. Utamuro has just uncovered the truth of a murder that had baffled everybody else.

First published in 1961, reprinted from the Doubleday Crime Club in 1982, *A Rush on the Ultimate* aspires to be a classic English mystery set in the Ambrose House Preparatory School, early in

September during a week of croquet matches between the Headmaster (the future murder victim) and his house guests, a group of stuffy, dreary, English upper-class stereotypes who number amongst their insular set, one lone outsider, an Australian, who gets constantly put down by a particularly obnoxious English matron.

Here's an example of what Cecily Ravell, the woman with the oversized bosom and the undersized brain, says to Ned Farron, the Australian: "I've no doubt that in Australia people don't particularly notice one murder more or less, but let me say that in some parts of the world the sanctity of human life is still valued" (149). Later, when Farron gets his "good suit" muddied by scrambling for Cecily Ravell's wretched Peke, all the thanks he gets is "Really, I should have thought an Australian wouldn't have been put off by a little dirt" (167). Predictably, most of these house guests (one of whom has surely bludgeoned his host to death with a mallet), try to pin the blame on the only two members of the lower class who have loyally ministered to their comforts: the housemaid, Rosalyn and the handyman, Bert Rogers.

There are a few Latin tags bandied about and there is a feeble attempt to give the whole an anthropological cast *a la* James Fraser, the Cambridge armchair anthropologist. As one of the house guests, a lecturer in classics, puts it, the headmaster, "provided a really startling instance of an age-old custom coming to life again in a contemporary setting. The dear chap was after all a clown. It is the only word, the obvious word. He was a physical fool..." (103). And as Ned, a fast learner, supplies the obvious corollary, the fool king is literally sacrificed and "whoever killed the Fool King succeeded to the throne" (105).

As in *Death and the Visiting Firemen*, the early Keating assumes that the reader is not bright enough to read character from the nuances of speech; he is impelled to supply redundant glosses. Here is a typical exchange between a father and daughter:

> "Daddy, I know we're going to pull off the doubles between us too. I feel it in my bones."
> Leonard looked down at her.
> "Don't be too confident," he said "You can make mistakes that way."
> A warning. (70)

One is continually amazed at the enormous chasm between Keating's early English mysteries and his later Indian ones. It is as if, after he abandoned the narrow constraints of English form and manners, his imagination found, in the variegated expanse of India, the space where he could find his own identity as a writer. His characters take flesh, his writing finds its own voice, his spiritual and philosophical concerns find the freedom to explore in the less obvious crevices of accepted truths.

The Dog It Was That Died (1962) is Keating's only foray into the genre of espionage and suspense, and takes its title from Oliver Goldsmith's poem which ends with the line, "The man recover'd of the bite,/The dog it was that died." Indeed, the only attractive character in this rather strange novel is the Irish Wolfhound, Cuchulain, who lunges at the evil professor, Bosenwaite, gets stabbed in the process, and saves his master, an escapee from the mysterious institute for brainwashing that the "Bosun" runs in Leeds.

This novel is unexpected on two counts. It is not a classic whodunit, nor even, as is usual with the later Keating, a parody of it. The would-be murderer is known to the protagonist, the mysterious Roger Farrar, who seeks to escape his past while the Bosun, the personification of evil, pursues him with the help of a brace of thugs. The novel is surprising not only for its departure from tradition, but because it is the most overtly political of Keating's novels. As the following dialogue between the Bosun and Farrar makes clear, there is more than an implied criticism of British imperialism:

> "Beat them all. That just about sums you up. That's the only way you know how to think. The new way of warfare. Britain must have the edge on everybody."
>
> "My dear fellow, are you saying that that shouldn't be so? Ireland must have softened your brain. Just think back to the fundamentals. You wouldn't want to see Russia winning a war, would you? Or America, for heaven's sake. Come, you must know Britain with all her faults, is the only power fit to be trusted."
>
> "The only power. That's the sort of blindness I sought refuge here from. Can't you see linguistics should never be part of a secret weapon? It's criminal to think in that way."
>
> "Linguistics for peace, eh? Ireland has done something to your mind. It must be the soft days, as they call them. The gradual seepage of fine mist into

the cerebellum. The sooner you come back to Leeds and a little realism the better. That sort of slogan stuff is simply one of the elementary tools of your own trade. You can't allow yourself to be deceived by it. It's like a master carpenter hitting his finger with a hammer."

"I didn't work for months on the uses of the word 'peace' without knowing it was a weapon, thank you very much. That's just why it took me so long to see it also meant something. It isn't only a word, you know: it's something that could exist. And the same goes for all the other words you so much love to see being monkeyed around with by stupid stooges like me. Well, I'm no longer a stooge. Ireland has done something for me, if you like. It's given me a chance to look at you from a distance."

"A distance? My dear chap, we shall have to give you some sort of rehabilitation course. You can't surely really think that Ireland is distant from Britain. Why, that's the crudest sort of propaganda put out in the pre-scientific days. You of all people can't have fallen for it."

"It happens to be true. Ireland actually is a different country from a colony you set-up over there."

The Bosun smiled.

"My dear fellow, Ireland is simply the last English eccentricity. Just wake up." (90)

This exchange illustrates the precise nature of British colonial attitudes. Ireland, like other colonies is subsumed under British identity. It would be interesting to speculate that Keating's years in Ireland where he graduated from Trinity College, Dublin, gave him a different perspective of British colonial assumptions. When Farrar says "Ireland has done something for me, if you like. It's given me a chance to look at you from a distance" (90), it is tempting to conclude he echoes Keating's own experience. Perhaps, *The Dog It Was That Died* foreshadows Keating's discomfort with provincial Englishness and his future escape to India in whose muddle he found a measure of freedom from British constraints.

Death of a Fat God features that redoubtable charwoman Mrs. Craggs, the sharpness of whose mind matches that of her tongue. As she goes about cleaning the provincial opera house which is the setting for the murder, not the slightest speck of dirt, literal or figurative, escapes her eagle eye. Naturally, she is the one to solve the murder of the new young soprano while her social betters cluck around helplessly like so many demented chickens.

Indeed, the cast of characters is suitably operatic, their emotions and behavior so exaggerated that they are almost caricatures. And what is worse, they are stereotypes. There is the immense French baritone, Jean Artaban Pivione, whose ego is as overweight as his body, whose malice is impartially directed at assorted mistresses and ex-wives, but who is kept on a short leash by his present wife, an American millionaire. There is also the Spanish director, Don Francisco de Zayes Y Tamago, whose fractured English lends itself to the high notes of hysteria. Add a neurotic pianist, a brace of temperamental divas and you have a nice cauldron of emotions bubbling both on and off the stage during the Flinwich theatre festival.

The murder is as spectacular as the characters who are involved. Pivione has succeeded in creating a turbulent atmosphere by his antics—he tries to upstage his leading lady by refusing to stay dead in the last act of *Tosca*. During the next production, Prokovinski's *Death of a Fat God*, emotions spin out of control and climax in a suitably theatrical murder. Pivione, playing the role of the God is slated to descend in a splendid machine, but it crashes down and kills a very new, and very promising young soprano.

While Mrs. Craggs has a keen appreciation and knowledge of opera, her common sense never deserts her. She is the only one whose wits serve the imperatives of evidence and logic. Her friend and sidekick, Mrs. Milhorne, on the other hand, is so in awe of the world of so called "high" culture that her naivete functions as a sounding board; she plays Watson to Mrs. Craggs' Sherlock Holmes:

> "Yes," said Mrs. Milhorne, "I ain't never been able to make out what all that's about neither. Though I do know Jean Artaban's been creating about it something awful."
>
> "Lots of nonsense if you ask me."
>
> "Well, it may be and it may be not. An artist like Jean Artaban's got to live on his nerves, and when you're doing that a little thing can make an 'ell of a difference. I know. I got nerves, too."
>
> Mrs. Craggs looked around Franz Prahler's dressing room. Everything seemed to be in its proper place.
>
> "All the same," Mrs. Milhorne said, "What is this car they keep talking about? I thought the opera was meant to be in the real old-fashioned days."
>
> " 'Course it is. It isn't a motor car they mean. It's more a sort of chariot. The god comes down in it out of the sky."

"Oh, I see. Sounds a bit silly to me though."
"It's opera." (95)

The character of Mrs. Craggs is the only surprising departure from the traditional English mystery popularized by Agatha Christie and others during the golden age of the genre. *Death of a Fat God* boasts all the usual conventions: limited number of suspects, closed door mystery, least likely suspect turns out to be the murderer, bumbling policeman et al. However, by making the sleuth a charlady, Keating shows very early in his career what he later came to do so well—spoofing established conventions of the genre. In the past, detectives have been invariably men and upper class—Albert Campion, Peter Wimsey, Hercule Poirot, not to mention Sherlock Holmes—whose values and attitudes were unembarrassedly elitist. By endowing a woman from the working class with intelligence, honesty and a fearless integrity, Keating very early blazed the trail for offbeat detectives. Although Agatha Christie created a woman detective in the person of Miss Marple, even she did not go beyond the bounds of class constraints. Whether Keating's innovations reflect conscious political beliefs or not, they do point the way to the originality of his Ghote novels.

Is Skin-Deep, Is Fatal, as the title suggests, deals with the world of tawdry clubs, beauty pageants and the underside of London where men's dreams have the depth and sheen of plastic, where beauty is a matter of the most blatant illusion designed to appeal to a world where women are strictly a commodity to be bought and sold. Appropriately, when the novel opens, a sort of male Madame Bovary, London Police Constable Peter Lassington, is sitting in his drab flat, in the company of his dreary wife, pouring over the glossy ads of bikini clad lovelies in the women's magazines he ostensibly, and ignoring her protests, buys for his wife.

His salacious dreams are interrupted by a phone call: Fay, the owner of *Fay's Place* has been found dead. So begins Lassington's peregrinations through the seamy side of London as Fay's mysterious death is followed by the murder of the organizer of the Miss Valentine beauty pageant in which Fay's daughter is a contestant. The investigation is in the hands of Scotland Yard's Superintendent Ironside whose laissez faire manner conceals a ruthless intelligence and respect for facts.

While his underlings are getting lost in a murky sea of motives, Ironside arrives at the solution, in a manner strongly reminiscent of Agatha Christie's *Who Killed Roger Ackroyd*, by rigorously piecing together the available evidence. In the autobiographical essay for the *Contemporary Authors Series* (Vol. 8), Keating admits that the plot was "blatantly pinched from Agatha Christie" (172). Keating says that he wrote this very traditional or one could say very derivative mystery, after he published his first Ghote novel, *A Perfect Murder*, before he realized how much his life would be "entwined with Inspector Ghote's" (172).

The Strongman (1971), the first of the four straight novels Keating wrote in between producing a host of mystery novels, probes the complexities and dangers of power. The novel is set in an imaginary island, Oceana, off the shores of Ireland, which is in dire need of wresting freedom from the iron rule of a self-made plantation owner turned tyrant-dictator, Mr. Mylechraine. Michael Quine, a journalist, on a visit to the island where he grew up and where his brother is a doctor humbly ministering to the needs of the dictator, is caught up in an insurrection led by the strongman, Thomas Keig, a simple peasant-farmer of exceptional physical strength who also has the attributes of a born leader: strength of conviction, will and absolute fearlessness. But alas, and this is the thesis of the novel, through the long, steady and often discouraging guerilla warfare he leads against the tyrant (who uses whiskey, witchcraft and sex to keep his populace in addled subjection), Keig who starts out with all the virtues and integrity of a minor god, becomes increasingly ruthless in doling out punishments and begins to resemble the tyrant he overthrows. Lord Acton's dictum that absolute power corrupts absolutely echoes throughout the novel. Starting out as a prisoner of Mylechraine, the growth of Keig as a leader is meant to illustrate the thesis that successful opposition to a ruthless dictator calls for similar attributes.

The story is told from the point of view of Quine, the journalist, who while aiding Keig in the laudable aim of overthrowing Mylechraine and fighting the war side by side with him, ruminates on the nature of power. While he admires Keig, he is frustrated by his inability to fathom the workings of his mind: "The trouble was that no one could ever tell with Keig. I can lay claim to knowing him better than any of the others, but I never fathomed what went on behind those dark uncommunicative eyes. I never felt I was seeing the machinery" (215). Unfortunately, Keig remains as much a mystery to the reader as to the narrator, and what is more, the mystery does not excite any suspense as there is a curious quality of thesis-illustration to the novel.

The Underside (1974), Keating's next foray into straight fiction is set in Victorian London and explores moral dichotomies. Godfrey Mann, a successful artist, is drawn in opposite directions by the twin urges of the flesh and the spirit. On the one hand he compulsively seeks out prostitutes in the most squalid streets of Victorian London, plunging deeper and deeper into physical degradation, while at the same time he is drawn to a woman who is the very epitome of intellectual and moral perfection. Elizabeth, a physician, a feminist and social reformer provides the kind of marriage and domestic tranquility which Mann feels should keep him anchored to moral uprightness. But alas, in this reader's opinion, Elizabeth comes across as such a straight-laced, humorless, pontificating prig that staying married to her becomes a measure of Mann's moronic character.

His forays into the Victorian underworld of dirt, violence, and sexual perversity, reminiscent of Joyce's depictions of nighttime Dublin, ends up being a tedious echo of it. The climax of the novel where Mann reaches the very nadir of perversion by literally linking sex with dirt, reads like a schematic illustration of a classic Judeo-Christian formulation of the binary opposition between the flesh and the spirit.

The depiction of the carnivalesque Derby Day, during which Victorian morals and mores are turned upside down, is a little too mechanistic as is the structure of the novel, with alternating scenes of upper-class repression and underclass squalor and freedom. Again, like *The Strongman*, *The Underside* reads like the painstaking illustration of Keating's moral concerns, rather than as a novel with dynamic characters who engage you by their vividness first and only secondarily serve as vehicles for philosophical explorations. When Keating writes the Ghote mysteries, the constraints of form keep him from letting simplistic moral equations take over the dynamics of plot and character. Also, the very lightweight nature of the whodunit form allows for the saving grace of humor, which is entirely absent in *The Strongman* and *The Underside*.

A Remarkable Case of Burglary is a departure from the formulaic mystery novel. It can be more accurately described as a thriller or a suspense novel. There is no question of trying to answer whodunit; rather, it is a matter of holding your breath wondering will he, won't he (the antihero), pull off a burglary in a fashionable and prosperous street in London. The master of No. 53 Northbourne Park Villas is a stereo-typically unattractive Victorian *pater familias*. He guards his silver, his jewels, his family and his servants with zealous acquisitiveness shorn of any vestige of tenderness or understanding, with the help of periodic outbursts of temper. A city merchant,

> He believed to the core that the circumstances of his birth, as a gentleman and as the inheritor of a worthy fortune, entitled him to this good living, as they equally entitled him to exercise to the full the power that had come into his hands. He did not like to be crossed. (13)

The man who wants to break into this citadel of bourgeois ideology is the penniless, handsome, Irishman Val Leary, who catches the eye of a downtrodden kitchen maid cleaning the steps of No. 53 and decides that the seduction of the maid could be the preliminary to an assault on this stronghold of Victorian mercantile wealth. Indeed the novel is structured on the extended metaphor of a military manoeuvre. The second chapter describing the household at No. 53 begins with the sentence, "The general officer commanding a fortress town takes his precautions, even in piping times of peace" (13), and the book concludes with, "Night falls on the battlefield. The dead and the dying lie where the hazard of battle felled them.... The reek of battle lingers in the air, tomorrow to be dissipated" (185).

Val Leary recruits seasoned cracksmen to plan an elaborate siege on No. 53. The planning is meticulous, including the minutiae, the rhythms of the household, it is a veritable triumph of logic. Alas, the ascendancy of reason is constantly undermined by chance and by the unpredictability of human emotion and response. The laboriousness of the planning makes the novel equally laborious to read, because the action of the plot is all in Val and his cohorts' efforts to master an environment they did not create, and the constant foiling of their plans by unexpected turns in behavior. For example, the poor kitchen maid, normally putty in the hands of Val, suddenly turns obdurate and refuses to help him because the butler is unexpectedly kind to her and she doesn't want to do anything that would hurt him.

What saves the novel from total tedium is Keating's feeling for the intractability of human nature, his talent for depicting the way emotions constantly subvert and transcend various determinisms. There is also Keating's empathy for the underdogs, especially those who fall in the interstices of a brutally unjust society, but manage to preserve their humanity against all odds. The kitchen maid, Janey, for example, emerges as a fully fleshed human being both weak and strong, vitally alive in spite of the vise-like grip of her social and economic circumstances.

Finally, in Marxist terms, the assault on No. 53, a fortress of middle-class respectability, by the underclass of London, can be seen as a true class war. One cannot help rooting for the success of the criminals, such is the unquestioning smugness and arrogance of the bourgeois and the cruel injustice of the class system which keeps them in power and the rest in inhuman subjection. It is clear from the epigraph that Keating's novel is based on much painstaking research in such studies as Henry Mayhew's *London Labour and the London Poor*. Indeed, while there is an unbridgeable gulf, both in conception and execution, between Keating's novels set in England and India, *A Remarkable Case of Burglary* comes closest in spirit to the deep humanitarianism and psychological realism of his Ghote novels.

A Long Walk to Wimbledon (1978) is Keating's contribution to the fiction of dystopia. Like George Orwell's *1984*, Aldous Huxley's *Brave New World*, and more recently Margaret Atwood's *Handmaid s Tale*, *Wimbledon* is set in a distant post-apocalyptic future in which London, once the epitome of the civilized metropolis, lies in ruins, barely controlled by the Armed Police, devastated by fires and riots, at the mercy of predatory gangs. Unlike Orwell, Huxley and Atwood however, Keating does not target the dangers of totalitarianism, of the left or the right. His apocalyptic vision seems to be the result of the bourgeois horror of permissiveness, epitomized by the 1960s' addiction to sex, drugs and rock and roll.

Jasmine, the very essence of the 1960s' permissiveness, lies dying in South Wimbledon as a result of her excesses. She sends a message across to Highgate, where her ex-husband Mark is holed up in desperate, besieged seclusion. She begs Mark to come see her. Much against his will, muttering "Wife, wife, bane of my life," Mark, a schoolmaster, makes his way across the minefield of danger that London has become. The novel has graphic descriptions of a London populated by Happies, the descendants of Hippies, who are violent, vicious and worst of all unmotivated, who could be expected to do anything at all, at any moment, for no good reason. Mark's odyssey through the rubble, the garbage, the smoldering ruins, his encounter with the various defensive groups ranging from the religious to the totalitarian which have formed in strategic locations, to a dying wife recalls Ulysses adventures on his return home to his wife, Penelope, in Ithaca. There are various guides, including a comic Indian storyteller, who instill a measure of wisdom and cheer him onward, till at the very end Mark realizes that although he does not reach his wife in time before her death, he has learnt that his former exclusionary certainty was, after all, very life denying. As a result of his passage through the decaying, dangerous city he had learnt, "That he should never have clung as he had done, clung long obstinately and hysterically, to what he had seen as a right certainty. Whirling, mad and uncertain it was, but it was not to be rejected" (182). Further, although he does not arrive in time to comfort his dying ex-wife, the journey was not wasted, because he had gained the insight that, "the world was a mad world but that madness was something to be acknowledged and saved" (191).

Again Keating's vision is that of a nineteenth century liberal humanist. He does not advocate a radical, revolutionary solution to the ills of the world, but portrays one individual coping with the great tide of barbarism which sweeps over him and surviving with a measure of humanity intact. No millenarian reforms, only minor, relatively sane voices heard in muted triumph.

The Lucky Alphonse (1982) is another, rather quirky, example of "straight" fiction that Keating seems to feel compelled to write from time to time in between the steady output of his far more successful Ghote novels. He says he wanted to look at one thesis—of being caught in the middle of two opposing, equally strong forces—from three different angles: the novel is experimental in form, "written in the manner of a symphony with, say, three movements in place of a continuous story" (Series 176). The three stories have protagonists with names which are variants of Alphonse, which Keating borrowed from the mildly off-color joke about the waiter Alphonse being caught lying between the chef and the head waiter and the manager exclaiming, "Ah the lucky Alphonse, in the middle again."

The three stories deal with the sometimes tragic, sometimes comic situation of being in the middle of opposing forces. The first story subtitled *Andante*

appassionata is about Alfonso Noronha, a very happily
married diplomat who thinks that an affair with an
American girl will not upset the balance of his life. He
expects to keep both wife and mistress happy with
himself blissfully in the middle. However, "The Great
Afonso striding his tightrope and making intelligent
conversation as he goes" (45) inevitably falls off, with
disastrous consequences. This story is unusual for
Keating in the sense that he describes Alfonso's erotic
life with sympathy and with convincing imaginative
detail. While in *The Underside* he depicts an artist's
sexual life, particularly his compulsion to explore
what Victorian Society considers perverse, the first
story in the *Lucky Alphonse* does so without
schematizing human experience into such simplistic
polarizations as spirit/matter, light/dark, good/evil,
etc. so dear to western ontology.

The second story "Fonsy Noonan's Story"
subtitled "Scherzo Presto," is set in the underworld of
Dublin and portrays the efforts of a small time crook
Fonsy Noonan to survive in the middle between the
demands of the police and his comrades in crime.
Always on the brink of getting thrown in jail or
getting bashed in by his comrades for betrayal, he
manages to walk the tightrope between being an
informer and a criminal, while also successfully
entertaining the reader with the nerve-tingling
suspense of his activities on both sides of the law. As
always, Keating captures local color accurately and
amusingly.

The third story, "Alfons Neumayer's Story"
subtitled "Allegro giocoso ma non leggiero," shows
the wide range of Keating's geographical and political
interests. It takes us to an emergent African nation,

so small and so defenseless that it is constantly in danger of being overrun by the White Land (ruled by whites) in the South and the Red Land (ruled by communists) to the North. A Bavarian professor, Alfons Neumayer, is summoned to Orangeland by his former pupil, Prince Loulou Kgama, who is now Prime Minister, to serve as philosopher-advisor, in the tradition of King Dionysius sending for Plato. Prince Loulou, charming, witty, enlightened, keeps the balance between two wives, one traditional in dress but radical in politics (she is an informant for Moscow), the other very westernized, but finds it less easy to keep his two aggressive neighbors happy in the face of his efforts to nationalize Ovangoland's diamond mines owned by White Land. However, all ends well, thanks to Professor Neumayer's strenuous teaching that, "To each force, seemingly irresistible, there is an equal and opposite" (180). Prince Loulou puts this aphorism to work, and by playing off White and Red Lands against each other leads his country triumphantly along the path of peace, progress and democracy. As Neumayer wings his way back to Bavaria and a new academic term, he reflects with quiet satisfaction that he could possibly permit himself a small joke that the story about King Dionysius and Plato, although apocryphal, might have some modern counterparts.

George Eliot and George Sand living in pre-feminist times used male pseudonyms. Keating, writing in the decades of vigorous feminist debate, chose to write mysteries set in the Victorian era under a female pseudonym—Evelyn Hervey. *The Governess* (1983), *The Man of Gold* (1985) and *Into the Valley of Death* (1986) all feature Miss Unwin, an orphan who has made her way, step by laborious step, up the social ladder from kitchen-maid to governess, who can never resist the appeal of unsolved mysteries. Endowed with what were considered "masculine" attributes—sense of logic, intelligence and ambition— the redoubtable Miss Unwin investigates the murder of her master, an industrial magnate in *The Governess* and in *The Man of Gold*, the suspicious death of her next employer, a man so acquisitive, he hides gold coins under floorboards (shades of Silas Marner) and insists that he can only afford inexpensive tainted meat for his family. In *Into the Valley of Death* (the plot of which Keating acknowledges having "pillaged" from Philip MacDonald's story "The Noose"), the Victoria Cross, the Charge of the Light Brigade and the Crimean War all play roles in the tangled motivation for murder in an English Village.

In all three novels, Keating portrays Victorian preoccupations with propriety, property and military glory accurately, but without capturing the reader's fascinated interest. If we compare Keating's Victorian mysteries with Ann Perry's, for example, we can see how he falls short in imaginative intensity and satirical skills. Anne Perry uses her setting to explore the hypocrisy, the shocking squalor which lay under Victorian decorum and prosperity. Keating barely touches on such issues and the plot is pressed forward painstakingly and with tedious, predictable devices. Miss Unwin comes across as a bit of a prig in her moral uprightness, and while in *The Man of Gold* she is offered a chance for romantic dalliance, resists the temptation with her usual unassailable logic. All in all, these novels are of interest only as forming a part of Keating's overall ouevre.

Mrs. Craggs: Crimes Cleaned Up is a collection of stories featuring the charwoman, Mrs. Craggs, who first appeared in *Death of a Fat God*. The stories have been published in *Ellery Queen s Mystery Magazine* and other journals, and have been strung together around an on-going (fictional) interview between Mrs. Craggs' friend, Mrs. Milhorne, (who plays Watson to Craggs' Sherlock Holmes) and a TV reporter who is trying to do a feature on the unusual sleuth. Although Agatha Christie, Dorothy Sayers, P.D. James and others have used women sleuths, Mrs. Craggs is a truly original creation because, unlike her fictional sisters-in-detection, she is not upperclass or educated. Mrs. Craggs is a cockney, whose five senses are alert to any hanky-panky even as she wields her duster with conscientious vigor.

She is also intelligent, in awe of no one, and supremely confident of her deductive powers. Indeed, five of the stories illustrate Mrs. Craggs' superb use of her five senses to arrive at the truth of the various shenanigans she witnesses all too willingly. For, armed with her mop and duster, Mrs. Craggs has access to all the different echelons of society, from the Queen's garden party (to the smooth running of which she makes a significant contribution), to the editorial offices in Fleet Street, to the House of Lords. In contrast to her sturdy common sense and self-assurance, Mrs. Milhorne is affected, endearingly silly, constantly at the mercy of what she calls "me nerves." The two of them are a lovable pair and Keating's ear for dialogue and the details of locale ring precisely true and there is his usual eye for the empathetic gesture that redeems Hobbesian man.

Interview 1

Conducted at Keating's London Residence,
4 January 1983

Tamaya: In my article on *Inspector Ghote Breaks an Egg*
which I sent to you before its publication in *Clues*, I
mentioned that you were Irish. Later, I saw that you
were listed as British in *Twentieth Century Crime and
Mystery Writers*. You didn't correct me. Would you
solve the mystery? Are you Irish or British?
Keating: Well, I am Irish by birth. My father, no my
grandfather, came over from Ireland to Scotland. He
was a clergyman and so my father was born in
Scotland, but Keating is an Irish name. We had a tiny
bit of land for years in the South of Ireland. I am not
an Irish citizen, but I suppose I thought oh well, if
she said Irish, I am by race Irish and I'll accept that.
In some ways I think I am Irish, I mean, you know
there is an Irish strain in me, fantasy perhaps?
Tamaya: Do you come from a family of writers?
Keating: No, not really. Certainly my father's side
were not writers at all. My father got his notion that
to be a writer was the best thing in the world to be.
My middle name is Reymond, spelled Rey, and it is

Published in *Clues: A Journal of Detection*, 1984. Reprinted with
permission.

said, by the family and I suppose they can hardly have invented this, when asked at my christening why I was given this name, he replied, "It will look good on the spines of his books."

Tamaya: Why did you choose to go to Trinity College?

Keating: After the war it was very difficult to get into British universities. There were all the ex-servicemen wanting to, and my school academic record wasn't particularly good, and so it occurred to my father that maybe I would get into Trinity College, Dublin, and I did.

Tamaya: You were a crime critic for the *London Times* weren't you? Did you start out as a journalist?

Keating: I think I had this notion of being a writer, it had been implanted. When I went to college, I had been writing. There is two thirds of a juvenile novel somewhere. But when I got, I suppose, to a state of maturity, I said to myself, I've got nothing to say, so I don't want to be a writer. Then I had to think that college was finishing shortly and I knew I didn't want to be an academic. I could have, I suppose.

Tamaya: Why not?

Keating: You see Trinity College is very parochial in a way, and I had seen academics there who really spent their whole life talking in bars and being fascinating, and I could see myself doing this, and eventually getting a Ph.D. but never producing a book, just endless talk...

Tamaya: That sounds familiar.

Keating: I made a conscious decision that I wasn't going to do this, that I would make a good sub-editor, I don't quite know why, what I can do is write. So I thought I would become a journalist. I read one or two books about journalism and got it into my head that I would make a good sub-editor, I don't quite know why, what you call a rewrite man in the States. In all innocence, when I went for an interview over here for jobs, I said this, and they are hard people to come by especially with good education, because it's a thankless, miserable job, and so their eyes lit up, and I got the job. I was for 4-5 years a sub-editor doing that dull routine, sitting at the same desk every night, walking the same route from home to the very pavement stones. I liked it, I was a very good sub-editor, because I am reasonably meticulous and I've got reasonably wide knowledge, that's what you needed and I would write a bright headline. So bright headlines were all I was writing. I began to progress up the scale to what they call copytaster here, copytaster which meant you sat there reading the news that came in and deciding what was to be done with it. So I didn't write anything at all. Then I'd been married sometime and my wife was anxious for me to be more ambitious than I was. I used to say half mockingly that I decided what I was going to be was a gentle failure, and she wasn't having any of that nonsense. She said, why don't you write something. I said I haven't got anything to say and she said why don't you write a detective story, they don't say anything, I thought you liked them. So, OK, I wrote one and sent it round to a lot of publishers, and it came back and I wrote another.

Tamaya: Which one was this now?

Keating: You've never seen it, because it never appeared. Another which never appeared and then a third one, I think, yes it was the third one, I sent one to an agent, he liked it and said I think I can sell this, but he couldn't. Eventually, he sent it back and said

I'm sorry I've tried everywhere and no. And then I sent him the next one, and he sent that one back almost by return because it was written in a rather curious style; and he thought this wouldn't do at all, and it lay on the table with his letter and parcel, green paper, I can see it, and eventually I thought, oh this is nonsense, just don't accept defeat, so I pulled out his letter and wrapped it up and sent it off to Gollancz the crime publisher here and yes, it was accepted.

Tamaya: The third novel? What was it called?

Keating: That was called *Death And The Visiting Firemen*.

Tamaya: I read that.

Keating: You have. You remember it begins in this, I don't know what the technical terms is, is it elliptical, I think it is, prose that is to say rather like the directions for a film script. Dawn, an old fashioned carriage, full stop, then lights coming in behind a ship, full stop. I had actually written this just to give myself some notes to start on, and then I looked at it and thought this is rather nice, I rather like this and so I wrote the whole of the book in this style with dialogue, whatever, and this attracted Victor Gollancz' fancy. It was new and fresh and different. They are hard to read for a reader who is not prepared to put a little effort in, because they think where is the verb? In fact, one of the great moments of my writing life was when I got a return from my agent and saw a small sum for an extract from *Death And The Visiting Firemen* used in so and so's English course. I thought, oh, my writing is being given to these school children as an example on how to write. So I rushed out and bought this English course for rather more money than I got from what they paid for it and there was this passage with the sentence underneath it: replace the verbs in the above passage, so this was no contribution.

Tamaya: How did you have enough patience and endurance to try and write another book and send it out? You wrote two before the 3rd was published. How did you keep going? You were working as a copywriter then.

Keating: Yes. I had a job, this was all done in my time off. Very largely because my wife had faith in me. And I suppose partly due to this notion which my father talked about a bit excessively that to be a writer was the greatest thing you could be, which is what I still believe. Yes, I don't want to be the Prime Minister, I want to be a recognized writer.

Tamaya: That seems to me the only decent thing to be. How did you manage to write these novels during your off hours?

Keating: Partly, I feel a bit guilty about this, being a sub-editor in London, I was on the *Telegraph* and then the *Times*, you worked in the evenings. I would come home around midnight sometimes even later, and sleep a bit late in the morning and then wake up fresh and write a couple of hours in the morning, perhaps a bit longer, and then slightly exhausted from writing, would go into the *Times* and give them the fag end of my brain.

Tamaya: You said you chose to write a detective novel because that is the one way you could think of writing without saying anything. Were you being facetious?

Keating: I was misguided, but serious at the time. I mean I thought, yes, a detective story just is a detective story: has a murderer, the suspects, the detective and the plot and just to do it and there is something to be said for this. When I talk to writers' groups as I sometimes do, beginning writers, I say to them if you feel you want to write, but you don't know what to write, think about a classic detective story because you get this framework which is very helpful to you. I wrote these first three on that understanding, but they were just games and they weren't really saying anything, and perhaps this is why the first two never got published because they were OK, but not as good as they might have been. It was only when I saw that first book, actually physically saw the book itself that I suddenly realized, of course, you could use this form to say things you felt and I thought what are the things I feel strongly about and one of them was, telling lies. As a child, you are told you must never tell lies and then you discover that people actually do tell lies. I can actually remember a traumatic moment in my life. I had been out with my father in the car, a drive going somewhere and he had shot a red light, and there happened to be a policeman standing on the far side and he pulled him over and said "Didn't you notice the red light?" and my father said, "No, I didn't" and his name was taken and he was to be summoned. Then we came back home, it was summer and we were having tea, typically English fashion, on the lawn under the cherry tree and my father started to tell my mother what had happened, and as he told this story it was obviously not in any way his fault, there was every good reason for him to have shot this light.

Tamaya: How old were you then?

Keating: Eight. I can remember this was the moment when father, the God, was revealed as having leaden feet. I can see this scene now. It was something I always worried about. So I thought this is ideal for a detective story, of course, and at the same time Zen was very much the thing being written about. And I saw that that, too, reflected on lies very much. I knew practically nothing about Zen; I read up 2 or 3 books and got a notion of how I could use Zen for a detective story. I did say something about lies, and each time I wrote I saw how much more I could say. Now I have perhaps got to the point where I say too much. But there are limits as to what you can deal with, what theme you can take.

Tamaya: Are you saying that the form itself has its limitations, or would you consider the possibility that the form is now taking a new turn?

Keating: Yes. I think the form has taken a new turn. I'm disconcerted to find that actually Dorothy Sayers took it many years ago. I suppose she knew what she was doing, but I don't think people by and large realize what she had done. Some people said, oh, she has converted the detective story into the novel of manners, but she had done more than that; she had converted it into a book that said something about a considerable aspect of the human dilemma. And I'm not the only one who writes detective stories like that.

Tamaya: When and how did you decide to switch to Ghote? I know you have answered this many times.

Keating: Yes. I have. We'll do it as briefly as we can. I would genuinely say there are two things that put me onto Ghote. One was that these books that I was writing were not getting published in America. You can imagine a book set, oh well, the second one, the Zen one, *Zen This Was Murder*, was set in a weekend adult residential college and I had been to such places and I described them pretty much the way they are and it's not a very romantic setting or anything. Very British, very typical of its type, and so one can see that American publishers were perhaps right to steer clear of that. And then I had others set in more or less similar very English settings that I happened to know about and not typically English, but just English. They were not getting sold in America, and if you are not sold in America, you cannot possibly make a living out of writing crime stories.

Tamaya: Does that mean that people don't buy books here as much as they buy in America? Why?

Keating: You can be a best seller in England and make a living, but you cannot be a best seller writing detective stories. The market just doesn't exist, you need sales abroad. So my first thought was I must avoid any of these very English settings. I am not sure that at that time I didn't toy with Russia, but it wouldn't have been because this was the height of the McCarthy era and it wouldn't have been a very clever thing to write about Russia. India was *in* that year. Do you remember when the invasion of Portuguese Goa was? I don't remember. Anyhow, the shining light was still there to some extent and so I was attracted to India for that reason.

Tamaya: Could we backtrack a little? The shining light, what exactly do you mean?

Keating: That India, certainly in the British press, was held up as being a fine example of neutrality, in the British liberal press. People thought, can there be a way out of the cold war and India a line between?

Simultaneously, one of the other things besides lies which obsessed or bugged me was perfectionism. Should you do things perfectly or settle for second best?

Tamaya: Why did that topic concern you? Are you a perfectionist?

Keating: I am a perfectionist in aspiration but in achievement I am a second best. I am born with a conscience; determined always to do the right thing. So perfection comes from that. So this was one of the possible themes that was in my mind. I am sorry to say that I thought of India as being marvelously imperfect, which in many ways it is.

Tamaya: How did you get that notion though, just from reading about it? Or from talking to people? Where did your mental image of India come from?

Keating: Yes. I do know where. I had cousins who were in India, an uncle who was a government engineer in India and two of my boy cousins were born and brought up there.

Tamaya: Where exactly in India?

Keating: I don't know. All I do know is we would get Christmas cards and my aunt, my mother's sister, was a very neurotic, forceful lady, who insisted that her poor servants should send me Christmas cards. Then I would talk to them when they came back from India and they had the full British stereotypical attitude toward India. I can remember them saying that Indians are silly, you know, they don't know that they ought to tuck their shirt tails in. But when first I went to Bombay and saw everybody with their shirt tails out, it was so hot, I did the same myself. I suppose it was from them that I got the notion of the inefficient Indian. When I was thinking, could I write about India and then I wanted to write about imperfection and I suddenly thought, oh, India land of imperfections. Marvelous. The final thing that set me off happened in this room. We were invited to a party, and some friends who live near by were supposed to give us a lift. We had no car then. Three friends came in, and with them was this chap who was just back from Bombay. He had been in advertising there. He had enjoyed India very much, but he wasn't dazed. You know you get the Englishman who unthinkingly praises every aspect of India, but this chap had his eyes open, and was able to say that things could be awful and this, that, and the other. Yet he had enjoyed his time very much in India. So I said to him, on the spur of the moment, that I was thinking about writing a book set in India. He was very very enthusiastic, and said that he would give me any help I needed. I really then did decide at that moment that I would do it.

Tamaya: Didn't the project alarm you, writing about a country you had never seen?

Keating: You don't really know what you are letting yourself in for, I mean, India to me then really was just one notion of somewhere where things were largely inefficient. That's what I wanted. I really knew so little about it. I hadn't noticed that Bombay was the best place, I really had to look at the map to make sure. I wanted to call him Inspector Ghosh simply because Ghosh, surprise, open wide eyes. And this chap when I sent him an outline, he said fine, but you cannot really call him by a Bengali name if he is to work in Bombay. He suggested Ghote, which is a very good name because in some ways it's a very typical Maharastrian name, but there are not a lot of them and also it, by chance, turned out not to be one of those police names. So from that point of view it was good. The English, of course, don't know how to pronounce the name, which is a constant difficulty.

Tamaya: Why didn't you accent the last syllable?

Keating: I suppose it's convention not to.

Tamaya: In India you mean?

Keating: Yes. Well, Indian names are reproduced in English in the newspapers or wherever, without accents partly because accents are a complication for printers. Yes, I did wonder whether to do it. Now I try to say it in the blurb, "you pronounce it GOTAY" which is not quite correct, but it helps. That was the strictly commercial part of Ghote. I was really extraordinarily lucky that I apparently could put myself in the mind of this sort of person in India and it's only just fanciful to say that I saw a blue streak coming from Bombay and landing on my head in London or as Indians have said to me you must have been an Indian in your previous life.

Tamaya: Until you wrote that book, you hadn't really known any Indians?

Keating: Hardly. No, there was an Indian journalist that I am now very good friends with. I just met him before I wrote the book or just after. But otherwise, I don't think I knew a single Indian.

Tamaya: Do you remember the Indian businessman you have in *The Perfect Murder*? He is so true to life. Gross and overbearing.

Keating: There is indeed a nice chap studying at a university here, who wrote to me and said he is just like my uncle. When I decided I was going to write about India, I took the time off, more time than I would take for a book, and I read as much as I could easily lay my hands on about India. I did a lot of reading, yes. Sometimes I think that's the only benefit I got out of a university education, the ability to take things from other people's novels and factbooks.

Tamaya: Who were the greatest influences on you?

Keating: I used to read as a boy a lot of detective stories. I liked them. I probably at some stage read nothing else. My mother was a great reader of detective stories. I would say they would be Dorothy Sayers, Michael Innes, Gladys Mitchell. The ones we liked were the really classical English ones. So they obviously are an influence. I am not now influenced, so to speak, by anybody and don't see myself writing books like so and so.

Tamaya: When I talked about influences. I was also referring to books on India.

Keating: Writers on India, yes. R.K. Narayan, of course. I liked Ruth Prawar Jhabvala very much. Now I think I have become more chary, she writes very well and very sympathetic books in a way, not perhaps sympathetic to India, but just sympathetic to her characters. I suppose I probably read Forster again in those days. Every time I go to India I come back with a suitcase full of paperbacks, Indo-Anglian paperbacks.

Tamaya: You didn't mention Naipaul. Are you a fan of his?

Keating: No. I'm not.

Tamaya: I'm so glad to hear that.

Keating: Partly. Because he is so prickly about India.

Tamaya: He is prickly about everything.

Keating: Yes. Also, I found him, by and large, ungrateful as a writer. The early novels I like very much. But certainly in *An Area of Darkness* and any of the factbooks, I find them quite difficult to read and unpleasing. I don't know quite why. I see that he probably has perceptions.

Tamaya: To return to your work, which is your favorite novel?

Keating: I think *Trusts the Heart* is my favorite.

Tamaya: I loved it, too.

Keating: I suppose it's the warmest; the subject gave full scope to that.

Tamaya: How did you conceive of the theme?

Keating: Very simple. I was reading *The Times* one morning and I am naughty with newspapers. I never read the leading articles; I read the funny bits. *The Times* doesn't have cartoons, but it has its own sort of funnies. Little snippets of news. And one of them, three lines, was that in Japan, Tokyo, I think, a rich man's chauffeur's son had been kidnapped and the people were holding him and asking for money. In a flash this seemed to be the most poignant situation and fascinating. I said to myself if I was that rich man just how much would I feel obligated to pay out for my chauffeur's son. For your own son presumably you would pay out as the Italian people do, every shilling you can lay your hands on, mortgage everything, but it really would be excessive to do that for someone else's child. So there was this whole broad dilemma.

Tamaya: I loved the book.

Keating: Good.

Tamaya: The businessman there is not as much of a caricature as the businessman in *The Perfect Murder*; he becomes human at the end. There is a flash, at least, of compassion in him.

Keating: He had to figure much more in the book, I mean, than Lala Varde, who was really just an obstacle in *The Perfect Murder*.

Tamaya: Could you go into more detail about how you start a novel and prepare for it?

Keating: It could have been two or three years earlier that I clipped this three-lined bit from the paper, thinking that's a marvelous idea for a Ghote book. When I finished whatever I was doing, I then, towards the end, would look at such ideas and say what should the next one be and to some extent if the one before had been more funny than anything else, then I would want to do the next one more tragical, whatever. If the one before had been set in London, I would think I must go back to Bombay again. So all sorts of technical things like that and then I would say, all right, I am going to do this one, then I would start working with it, reading anything relevant or just general Indian books.

Tamaya: When you open a notebook, what sort of things do you jot down in it?

Keating: Two strains, one is subject notes which is anything to do with a particular aspect of India that I am writing about, and then method, which is anything to do with the actual way I am going to write the book. I mean, it will occur to me that such a thing reflects the theme, or I ought to have a character of such or such a sort.

Tamaya: Do you at any time think, "I am spending too much time thinking about it, I should get to my task and write"?

Keating: Oh yes you do, I mean I do. I have to sort of force myself to go on thinking. One of the things a writer has to acquire is what I call charge, and you can do that by being a genius, in which case you already have a great charge behind what you write, or you can do it by using a lot of time, by thinking for a long time about your subject. Something reminds me of some particular Ghote book I thought of writing. For a moment or two I think about it and then it goes to the back of the head and things happen there.

Tamaya: When you're thinking about it, do you mean to say you are just walking around the house thinking about it all the time, is that how it works, or is it more or less on an unconscious level? I know you are reading and taking down notes.

Keating: In the period, in these next three months, or whatever, I, yes, I said, I am reading, then I'm taking a note, but I also will have occasional spells of suddenly thinking oh, there is this subject of the book and I will write questions to myself and try to think of the answer or I will go out and walk and try and say to myself when I go out I must be thinking what sort of a person will such and such be. Having written pages of subject notes and pages of method notes, I then take a page or more for each character and generally write their age or something just to force myself to think about them and what is the most obvious trait of their personality. Also, I allocate pages to the chapters. When I began I was terrified I wouldn't have enough to make a book long enough, so I wrote down what I thought each chapter would be. Now I find, mysteriously, I do all right, seem to write the exact length without having to think and about it, but I have written down about 20 chapters.

Tamaya: And you work in the morning for a couple of hours?

Keating: No. I work every day from 9:30-6.

Tamaya: You are actually at your desk writing from 9:30-6.

Keating: I am actually in the study alternatively writing and flopping back and reading, I can write for about half an hour at the most. So then I read a few books, which at times I feel a bit guilty about because when I am exhausted I start to read and assess someone's work, but a crime book is easy. It isn't as if you are reading a complex work on the imagery of Shakespeare.

Tamaya: So you write for half an hour and then read for half an hour or whatever, and then another spell of writing. And when you read, you read someone else's book.

Keating: At first I thought this was dangerous, you know, would I go back and write Ghote and turn it into a Chandler character, but no, you can switch the mind, or I can.

Tamaya: Which is your least favorite book? Which did you think was your worst novel?

Keating: For different reasons, my least favorite books are *Murder of a Maharajah* and *Go West Inspector Ghote.* *Murder* was written much too fast, at what I thought was a superficial level. And *Go West* because America or California was too much for me I think. I ought to have spent longer there, seen it quietly for myself and then I might have been able. British critics complain that the picture of California was very, not crass but rather simple, the jibes I made, and perhaps thus, it was.

Tamaya: In *Murder of a Maharajah* game playing figures largely. Could you talk about your interest in game playing?

Keating: Only mildly interested in it, but, I suppose, in fact, from watching, slightly appalled, my own children, who seemed to spend an inordinate amount of time playing any sort of game: pool, board games. They would spend hours playing. I was very struck by it, and I don't think as a boy I used to spend that much time. I do occasionally play something, but it's enough for me on the whole.

Tamaya: When you talked about game playing, you literally meant games, you didn't mean role playing.

Keating: No, role playing, no. Frivolity, reading detective stories, in a way, in that book I do refer to an Agatha Christie detective story. But they are time wasting, yes. I was fascinated by how people can spend a lot of time on frivolities of that sort, and, in a way, the Maharajah was a person devoting his whole life and huge sums of money to playing games and practical jokes of various sorts.

Tamaya: What about the sapura bark? I have never heard of that. Is that a piece of fact or fiction?

Keating: It is fiction, yes. I am very proud of it. It is a sort of a tribute to the writer's imagination that you can produce things which are "factier" than fact.

Tamaya: It's wonderful. Marvelously inventive.

Keating: It's just a word. I got it out of my head. I needed this stuff that would block the part of the gun. Originally, this was once upon a time going to be a film script for James Ivory. He asked me on the day of the memorial service for Agatha Christie, because I went from there to have lunch with him and he said would I write it. He wanted for once to do a really popular film, would I write it, set in India.

Tamaya: Why didn't you make it into a film then?

Keating: Oh, because he and his friend Ismail Merchant work very rapidly and as soon as they finish one project they must start another, for they need the money and they look around and this happens to be in the forefront and they do it. And so, it so happened when I sent him an outline for this he was busy on a film and he said to me, I've carried our letter in my pocket for six weeks and he did write and say thank you, but it just happened to hit at the wrong moment, so I think they would have had difficulty getting the financing for as big a picture as this would have been.

Tamaya: Have you thought of sending it to any Hollywood producers like Sidney Pollack or Sidney Lumet?

Keating: It was with a man called Robert Soho, who made *Invasion of the Body Snatchers*, and he laid it off with Universal. I got a lot of option money for it. Universal was taken over by some other big film people and what happened was they immediately cleared out all the front office staff and any projects that are going, they abort instantly. And this is what happened to mine. They had a script written by Anthony Shaeffer.

Tamaya: Where exactly is your script now?

Keating: Somewhere in Hollywood presumably. I mean they paid for it. No, the option came to an end so my agent could sell the option again. I suppose Shaeffer's script belongs to Robert Soho or whatever and will moulder in a drawer forever.

Tamaya: And you could never send it to anybody else?

Keating: If someone else got interested in it and took an option, I suppose he would tell them there is a Shaeffer's script and I guess they then could buy it, if they were let, from whoever he wrote it for. Hollywood is just so extraordinary, the absurd things they do. I mean, it is a standard thing to buy a book on an option written by somebody or other and fly people out from Britain for half an hour's conversation. They really paid me a very large sum you know.

Tamaya: For the option?

Keating: For the option, yes. But I had been paid small options for things, and my agent said to me, don't for heaven's sake think they will ever make this film because they are not the sort of company that could make a film or would make a film of one of your books. But let's have this little bit of money.

Tamaya: I'm curious to know why when you talked about your least favorite novel or novels you didn't mention *Filmi, Filmi Ghote* which I thought was worse than *Go West*.

Keating: Yes. There are little bits of it that I liked I think and yes, as I look back on it, something did go wrong, it was sort of too crude, the satire was too crude. But I suppose the reason I still have some interest or faith in it is that I put so much mental capital into it that I can't bear to write it off.

Tamaya: You're saying you didn't like *The Murder of the Maharajah* because you didn't work too much on it, but you liked *Filmi, Filmi Ghote* because you worked a lot on it.

Keating: Well, yes, yes. You know I feel it is wrong for a book to be good unless you've done a lot of actual work on it.

Tamaya: To change direction a bit, in a longish essay I wrote on you for an anthology on *British Mystery Writers* I made the connection between your philosophical outlook and that of Teilhard de Chardin. Was I very far off the mark?

Keating: Well, yes. I'll tell you what happened with Chardin. I was sort of vaguely aware of him and then by sheer coincidence an uncle of mine who is a businessman conceived the notion that he wanted to write something which would explain Chardin for a wide audience and he asked me if I would help him and said he would pay me for the work and I needed the money. In any case he was a charming man and I like him and so I agreed. I did quite a bit of work on it. And then he said to me when it was done he said, oh, your name shall be on this as well and I said no, no I really don't want it and he said you must so I said well, I'll tell you what, sometime when in other sorts of books they are described as being by Maurice Keating with so and so meaning this is the work of ghost writer, help or whatever—I said that would be a nice formula and so we agreed on this. It was convenient for the publishers to put it that way and so the libraries all over the world credited me with this book here.

Tamaya: How much of the actual writing did you do?

Keating: I should think quite a bit of it.

Tamaya: Well, then, it is just as well your name is on it.

Keating: Well, yes, but I mean it was largely paraphrasing: it was a journalist's job, I don't really want to take credit for it and I think it is coincidence if you can link any of his thoughts with my attitude towards life.

Tamaya: I'm sure it must be...your letter saying ignore it came after I had written the paper and I couldn't very well throw it out.

Keating: It makes sense once you say it, but I think it's actually not really so.

Tamaya: Your Ghote novels have three aspects, 1) the philosophical concerns, 2) the satirical portraits of India and Indians, and the third aspect is your mastery of Indian English. Which aspect do you think is the most important?

Keating: Well, obviously the philosophical theme. Because for better or worse I really think of myself as a novelist, and I'm using the crime form to say what I have to—I like using it, but I am using it. I'm slightly dismayed by your emphasis on the satirical because I don't really mean, most of the time, to be satirical about Indian life...I mean to be descriptive.

Tamaya: I suppose the truth is so funny that it fits.

Keating: Well, yeah exactly, I mean all right, I am conscious that you do that for a Western audience. You choose those aspects of Indian life that are amusing, different or whatever and yes, Indian businessmen are no worse than American or British businessmen, but they have a way of being bad that is different. With the *Filmi, Filmi*, I did: I mean those people are so absurd you have to treat them satirically.

Tamaya: That one book is very satirical.

Keating: Yes, I was saying earlier on that I think when I finish one book, I think what the next one will be. I thought a satirical one would be a sort of different one from whatever came before it. I owe an enormous amount to India. I owe all my success to India. I was quietly writing these books which were doing all right, but they weren't doing terrifically and they weren't selling in America and I feel I should have to thank India for this and I wouldn't like to think that I was mocking all the time, only occasionally. I can remember I was interviewed on television in Bombay and the interviewer asked me something like this and I said what do you mean being satirical about India. I am satirical but not about the whole of Indian society and indeed I go to some trouble always to have a balancing character.

Tamaya: Yes, you do. And that's what makes you so different from Naipaul or Jhabvala and very refreshing, because you try to see the other point of view, or you try to see it from another angle and you always imply that there are other angles. In my long piece on you I have said the philosophical concerns come first and that incidentally there are also satirical portraits. I stressed the philosophical concepts because, ultimately I see your novels as universal, about universal problems, human problems.

Keating: Yes. I hope that they are. I mean because they spring from my own concerns as a person about some aspect generally of my behavior. I think, there is the tension you get in any character between what is universal and what is exceptional, and my way of being exceptional is to write about Indians. But I think the one shows up the other. Every little bit of knowledge I have, I have to make it fit the story. Just this morning I wanted, sort of, three examples of the way Ghote's wife behaved. And I was able to think of three sort of typical Indian things for the Western reader's benefit.

Tamaya: How on earth did you grasp the nuances of an Indian woman's relationship with her husband? Do you know any Indian couples?

Keating: This is from books. Yes, I suppose I have seen it. There are some Indian couples I have come to know, more cosmopolitan. I think I only gradually came to appreciate women.

Tamaya: What does that mean?

Keating: You know when you are an adolescent, a young man, women are largely sex objects or you see them in a sexual relationship all the time. And it's only, in say the past ten years, that I began to see women as women but admirable, you know, without any sex thing. We were saying the other day, in fact about next Tuesday, it so happens that around the table there will be probably more women than men. This is because husbands can't come and things like that and I was saying to Sheila, I really wouldn't mind if it so turned out that we have a dinner party with me and seven women. I mean there will be seven interesting people. I would feel, now, that this is not in any way odd.

Tamaya: Why don't you describe your characters in physical terms? There are surprisingly few details of how they look in your books. Ghote, for instance, is physically very shadowy.

Keating: Ghote has to be because you are seeing him from what I call the angel on his shoulder point of view all the time. So you are not exactly looking through his eyes but you are more or less, so he doesn't see himself. Some writers do this always in the first chapter, I don't know if you noticed, have the hero look in the mirror and describe his face as he sees it. I didn't, I thought it was a bit of a trick. So, Ghote isn't described.

Tamaya: Neither is Protima for that matter. She is only described as elegant and pretty.

Keating: I think this is because I'm rather bad at seeing. Perhaps I don't look at women enough, that is I don't look at people enough, actually. Somebody once pointed out to me that in every book I have a very fat man. What does this mean, they said. I couldn't think what it meant, but I think actually now what it means is that I only notice extreme physical characteristics.

Tamaya: Not the other details. You mentioned your straight novels: how many have you written and why have you abandoned them?

Keating: I haven't abandoned them. One came out recently.

Tamaya: Which one?

Keating: It's called *The Lucky Alphonse*. It came out the October last. Not in the States. What happened was, well I suppose if you consider yourself a novelist, there must come a stage when you consider writing a novel and we had a publisher friend who said to Sheila, Harry ought to write a novel.

Tamaya: Why do people say you ought to write a novel? From hearing you talk, or have they read something of yours?

Keating: He had read and liked the Ghote books, but he wasn't publishing them and I think he thought he would like to publish this writer and said let him write a novel and we'll publish it. And so I did. I put a lot of emotional capital into it. But it didn't do very well. To begin with it didn't sell to America. If they don't sell to America they are an indulgence for me. It means that year I am going to make less money so I can't do it too often. I wrote yet another. You haven't read *A Long Walk to Wimbledon*? It's set in London when the worst has happened. It hasn't been atom bombed but riots and everything and it is a devastated city.

Tamaya: There are some excellent English novelists never heard of in America.

Keating: Yes. Even I, you see, in a rather pathetic way, put in bits to make them attractive to American readers.

Tamaya: What kind of bits?

Keating: Like *A Long Walk to Wimbledon*. I wanted some district, a man walks right across devastated London, that's a sort of picaresque novel from that point of view. So I thought what arena of London will be familiar to American, ah Wimbledon, and that perhaps is the only concession to Americans, and indeed, one of the people at my agents said that they thought it was too closely linked to London streets. I don't think that she is right because we read some American books that are very detailed about a particular area they are writing about and you are quite happy, or come to that, people will read about Bombay.

Tamaya: Would you say something about Mrs. Craggs? I love her.

Keating: Yes. She came to life after the last, yes, I think it was the last of the pre-Ghote books, and I got this notion of a down-to-earth charlady, being in a way because of her down-to-earthiness and physicality, a better detective than others. And I also wanted to write about opera and so this was a nice contrast, that of opera and the down-to-earth lady.

Tamaya: Are you fond of opera?

Keating: Yes. I don't go enormously, but yes. And so I wrote this one. There again you see if I set it in Covent Garden it might have sold in America, but I didn't know about Covent Garden, so I set it in, or rather made up a provincial English opera house having a short season. And so there she was and I was very happy with her, but then Ghote came along and obviously I must write about him. Then I was asked to write a set of short stories for radio, five short stories to be read, one each day. I thought how about doing her and then being five I called them *The*

Five Senses of Mrs. Craggs which brought out her earthiness very nicely. Then at odd times I've written short stories and sent them to *Ellery Queen Magazine*. Do you know Otto Penzler?

Tamaya: I don't know him personally, but I know of him.

Keating: He interviewed me like this and at the end of it he said he very much would like to produce a collection of her stories. This was in 1966 and I still haven't got around to producing enough stories. He's a very nice guy. He did produce that second addition of *Murder Must Appetize*. Very nice in a slick case, beautiful cover, whatever. So he hasn't totally let me down.

Tamaya: To turn to the subject of Indian English, how on earth do you have such a good ear?

Keating: I have a reasonably good ear for voices. I mean, Sheila and I, she has a particularly good ear for dialects and whatever, and so we will occasionally have conversations in Scottish or in Yorkshire or whatever. Yes, I think I've got an ear. Mind you when I say an ear, it's all from, mostly from reading Indian English, mostly in Anglo-Indian novels.

Tamaya: Mr. Ramaswamy, for instance, in *Ghote Goes by Train* speaks with a distinctive "Madras" accent. Did you get that from books too?

Keating: Somewhere I think I read it, and then I realized I heard it. It's interesting that what is good dialogue in a novel is not good spoken dialogue. I have a notebook in which I write down characteristic expressions. Just last year I came across this scholarly work produced by two Indians and a British scholar called *Varieties of Indian English*. What I do now, I read a few pages every morning before I start to write, to sort of get it into my head. I have eavesdropped on

Indians talking here and occasionally got some going to films.

Tamaya: Indian films?

Keating: Yes, of the captions. Especially when they are done in Indian, when they have subtitles, they use very Indian expressions which are marvelous.

Tamaya: I enjoy them so much.

Keating: It's nice, it's so characteristic. I think it was you who said there are three varieties. There is the cooley who speaks a word or two and then there is Ghote's type and then there is Oxford educated who tend to speak in a far more formal way. I think probably there are wider varieties, but I think it is too complicated to get into a book.

Tamaya: I particularly liked the book *Inspector Ghote s Good Crusade*. Did you like it?

Keating: Yes. I did it's now so long ago since I wrote it, it does begin to fade in one's mind. I have a friend, a nice man, who writes very unpretentious, good, but unpretentious crime stories. Michael Underwood, do you read Michael Underwood? You would like them I think. He was a legal officer and they are good. He doesn't claim to do more than write quite at a simple level, he doesn't put much of himself ever into books and doesn't want to and he says to me he really forgets the names of his characters almost as soon as he's finished the book. I hope that I don't do that.

Tamaya: I hope you don't do that. That is one of the reasons why I don't like Michael Underwood. His characters never really do come alive.

Keating: No, they don't. They are all right, they fulfill their function, but he doesn't aim to do more than that. Perhaps he's at his best when he sometimes gets a very interesting situation and then the books are good and then occasionally you get a flick of something good in a character which is interesting.

Tamaya: And Antonia Fraser, I am so disappointed in her. Did you read many of hers?

Keating: I did. I am so glad you said what you did. I did like *A Splash of Red*.

Tamaya: What about *A Remarkable Case of Burglary*? What were you trying to attempt in that?

Keating: That started out as a radio play, which we do much more than in the States. I had just written the book called *The Underside*, the Victorian novel. It's a novel, my second novel, it's called *The Underside* and set in Victorian London in 1870s. While I was doing it I came across a description about a burglary in a big house round about here which is fascinating. There again what was good radio dialogue wasn't right for book dialogue. And I also decided I could use the same story to write about chance, which is difficult to write about anyway and so, yes this was intended. Another factor was I wrote it just before I went to India for the first time. I didn't want to write a Ghote immediately before going to India because I thought I would see things there. So I filled in by way of doing this Victorian crime story.

Tamaya: I kept reading it with interest, but I wasn't sure what you were trying to do. It was so meticulous and ingenious, but there was something missing there.

Keating: That's interesting. I think you're right.

Tamaya: What was the point of it all? That wasn't quite clear.

Keating: Probably because it wasn't planned with that theme in mind.

Tamaya: But that did come across.

Keating: I had running through it, which I quite liked, sort of a big running image based on a sort of romantic war image as if it was *War and Peace* sort of fighting and I think I used that to point up the chance element.

Tamaya: Did you get good reviews?

Keating: Yes, it did. In the States it did well, it came during the *Upstairs, Downstairs* thing and took advantage of this. Again, I wrote it to fill in time.

Tamaya: Are you working on a new book?

Keating: Yes. I started thinking about a new Ghote novel on January 3rd (82). I started writing about October 1st.

Tamaya: I am glad a new one is coming out. I shall look forward to it.

Keating: One evening, one short evening next year you will be able to devour it.

Interview 2

Conducted at Keating's London residence,
26-27 June 1990

Tamaya: Since I've just finished reading your most recent novel, *The Iciest Sin,* maybe we could just begin with that. I notice that you have romanticized the Parsee community as a whole. Do you have a particular fondness for Parsees?

Keating: I have a romantic notion about...oh, most things, probably wildly inaccurate, but I'm apt to have romantic notions about certain people or class of people. My father was a great romantic, was having tremendous notions, like for instance, he took me out of school at age 16 and decided I was going to the university of life, which possibly was a good idea. But all my contemporaries were staying on in school and were going off to University and I went to college because I got a government grant after being in the army.

Tamaya: Um. That's interesting. Parsee names are generally associated with business—Baltiwallah, Paperwallah, etc.—it is hard to think of business as romantic or noble.

Keating: Perhaps not. Noble is not the right word. Two things impressed me about the Parsees: beginning from a lowly place and by sheer effort rising up. My hero was Edgar Wallace, who was a

Published in *Clues: A Journal of Detection,* 1992. Reprinted with permission.

foundling more or less, looked after by a fish porter and his wife who by sheer dint of hard work rose up to be...They say eventually one in four books of his was a best seller. Though he is rather a rotten writer, he is someone I admire. The Parsees are the same way, risen up by effort. Plus their philanthropy—I have managed to work that in.

Tamaya: Both *The Iciest Sin* and *Under the Monsoon Cloud* deal with Ghote violating the police code. In *Monsoon Cloud* he helps the murderer dispose of a body and in *The Iciest Sin*, he does something unthinkable—he witnesses a murder and decides to let the murderer go free—I was outraged. It does not seem plausible.

Keating: You were outraged by *Monsoon Cloud*?

Tamaya: I found it hard to believe that Ghote, who has been portrayed as the one incorruptible officer in a largely corrupt police force, should behave as he does. It is not as if he has been built up as a crooked cop...he is always consulting Hans Gross' *Criminal Investigation*. If anything, he's overly, boringly, conscientious. How could he possibly become an accessory to murder?

Keating: Because he is a human being. I asked myself what I would do in a terrible dilemma.... I know that probably I wouldn't do necessarily the right thing. The human weakness that I think you ought to have to offset the heroic. Ghote, for all that he is small scale, is heroic.

Tamaya: Makes him more human then?

Keating: Yes, yes. But in the *Monsoon Cloud*, having done that, having virtually put Ghote on trial for it, I continue to bring in a post-verdict, if you like, which exonerates him, thereby saying, yes, I think in the circumstances, he did the right thing. Every dilemma is an individual dilemma and uh...you can't produce a rule to say you will do this every time. I mean the origin really of *Inspector Ghote Draws a Line* down from this. I was thinking about people declaring: so far, no further. I was at that time working for this *Catholic Herald* paper—in those days I was still a Catholic—I remember the Cardinal Archbishop of Westminster was declaring that there was some line you couldn't go past. I was introduced to him. All we did was chit chat about television but all along I felt I should be challenging him. So two years later, I wrote *Draws a Line*.

Tamaya: It is rather like E.M. Forster saying—I am paraphrasing—if I had to choose between a principle and a friend, I would choose a friend.

Keating: Yes, yes. I think that does say I would choose an individual, each case is an individual case. Although one has principles which apply most of the time I think one has to be always aware that there may come a time when principles are overridden.

Tamaya: Do you see yourself in the tradition of the 19th Century English moralists?

Keating: Oh yes, yes. Very much so. One of my editors was always ribbing me about being a moralist. I think you are perfectly right that I am in the Forster tradition.

Tamaya: Yet, in *The Iciest Sin*, Ghote in effect thinks that Dr. Commissariat is so admirable that it is all right for him to commit a murder. That's a little hard to swallow—I mean, after all, murder is the ultimate crime....

Keating: Yes, yes. You will see that my editors found it a little hard to swallow; they put in a little qualification or a few words of excuse. I wanted to present the sort of utmost dilemma I could find for Ghote, and this, it occurred to me, was. The whole book does put that in a different light.

Tamaya: In *Under a Monsoon Cloud* Ghote realizes that Kelkar's rages are not necessarily the best way to solve problems.

It seemed to me that because the murderer in *Sin* has already stolen a thesis, has entered the penthouse of the blackmailer prepared to murder, he is really a very cold-blooded, super-efficient murderer. He tries to rationalize away his crimes by telling himself and Ghote that he is doing it all for a noble cause: philanthropy. I really can't see how Ghote could have bought the murderer's version of himself.

Keating: Yes. Well, for one thing I'm apt to take people at face value myself. And indeed, I probably took the whole Parsee community at face value. Coming to write about them I prepared to put in some bad parts as well. I mean, it just never occurred to me that Ghote should have questioned whether Commissariat was a wholly good man. From the point of view of the book, fiction/fact, I declare with authorial authority, he is the model of a good man.

Tamaya: This brings me to a really interesting point. You kept talking about Ghote's moral dilemma as the kind of thing *you* might face, and what *you* might do under the same circumstances. In other words, you place before Ghote problems you would like to explore yourself....

Keating: Yes. Well...I'm afraid I *might have* to explore.

Tamaya: Yes. Through Ghote you explore those moral issues and Ghote responds as *you* would. That is fascinating because you have made a clear identification between your psychological make-up and Ghote's.

Keating: Yes. I think it is there.

Tamaya: I want to look at this from another angle here and talk about Edward Said's seminal study of Western formulation of the East as the mysterious Orient.

Keating: Yes. I have read reviews about it.

Tamaya: Said argues that the West has projected its own worst fears and fantasies on the Orient which is cast in the role of the alien Other. Has this happened to you in your Ghote novels? Did setting your novels in India liberate you from the constraints of British norms, so that you are free to imagine, to break the boundaries of what is considered quintessentially British?

Keating: Yes. I think you are right, I wrote three crime novels set in Victorian England and this is the same thing. I like to observe from a distance. I like to go back in time and space. I did three of them. My agent persuaded me to do them. She said they would sell better than the Ghote novels because Ghote in those days was not selling in paperbacks. And I got quite interested in doing them. They didn't do all that well, so I abandoned them. I'd be interested to find what you feel about the novels.

Tamaya: I found they were very hard to get through; they were very slow reading. The first time I read the *Remarkable Case of Burglary*, I couldn't bring myself to finish it. But the second time around I found it interesting in terms of the class struggle. The metaphor of siege runs right through the novel and this huge house, emblematic of Victorian bourgeois capitalism is besieged from the outside by the underdog of all underdogs: the burglar is a poor, out-of-work Irishman. Because the Victorian *pater familias* is such an awful autocrat, the book seems to be an indictment of patriarchy, capitalism et al.

Keating: Yes, yes. But the characters are stereotypes and as I was attempting a wider market, I was using stereotypes, but it never occurred to me that it was slow. I suppose one has one's blind spots.

Tamaya: One of the interesting things about the book is that you made the maid Janey transcend the stereotype. Here she was seduced by the Irishman into being disloyal to the family she works for, but she recovers her loyalty when the butler is kind to her. There the interpersonal cuts across socio-economic determinism.

Keating: Yes, yes. What happened was, as I wrote I got more into the stereotype, I saw her as a unique human being.

Tamaya: You often do that...in the way human beings defy expectations...transcend their socio-economic circumstances. In the end these responses are unpredictable. That adds suspense to the novel.

Keating: Yes, yes. You use it to add plot twists to the novel.

Tamaya: To get back to stereotypes...Dennis Porter, in his comparison of the British Golden Age mysteries and American hard-boiled novels talks about Agatha Christie's affection for stereotypes, as the limitations of her social class. If a murder is committed, it is an infringement of law and order which is restored to its status quo. In his words: "In its broadest sense the landscape, the style, the hero are emblematic of the deeply conservative ideology of golden age mysteries." Now it seems to me you do not quite conform to this pattern. The landscape is, of course, Indian, an unknown landscape with incredible variety, and you often move from city to country: a classic Shakespearean dialectic. There is a critic who talks about mysteries as being structured along the same lines as Shakespearean comedy.

Keating: Yes, yes. There is some truth in that. Except that Shakespeare isn't really the starting point. It goes deeper than that. The starting point is the human psyche.

Tamaya: Do you really think the culture/nature opposition is deeply rooted in the human psyche? Dennis Porter points out, quite rightly I think, that it is typically British to regard culture as origin of law and order whereas in America the wild west is where you find freedom and purity. The California city, Los Angeles, for instance, is the hub of all corruption.

Keating: The fundamental theory this arises from is order and chaos.

Tamaya: Yes. But a Marxist critic would say that the establishment usually creates and imposes its values and then goes on to say that values are not socially constructed but human, innate, natural values.

Keating: Yes, yes. Just like Mrs. Thatcher pretends her conservative values are natural and universal. But

I think that whatever rationale is given to this, these are things that come from the deepest human instincts that all human beings at times want to live in order, and, at times, want to venture into chaos.

Tamaya: The so called binary opposition which the post-structuralists have so effectively deconstructed.

Keating: I don't think that they are—I really do think that the psyche has these opposites. Everybody shares them.

Tamaya: To go back to the *Sheriff of Bombay*, first it seemed to me that the prostitutes in the red light district were wonderfully varied...They did not conform to any one stereotype. Some actually enjoyed their profession. Some were abused, victimized and so on...Every one of them had an individual point of view, an individual voice.

Keating: Yes, yes. Partly because oh I think.... One reviewer said typical golden hearted whore...I resented that. I was very determined, writing about prostitutes to write about them as they are in life. I was lucky I got hold of a couple of books. One written by an Indian sociologist who interviewed prostitutes and one by an American photographer. And so I was able to find real life examples.

Tamaya: Did you tour the red light district when you were in India?

Keating: I did. Indeed I was taken there by the police. You know they like to show off the cages. They have made them into a tourist attraction. They said to me, would I like to go round. I thought, do I really?...I had no idea about it...I felt I had to be polite and said yes...Indeed it was fascinating....

Tamaya: Really? Wasn't it depressing? It must have been.

Keating: No, no. It wasn't depressing. Because we went to an opium den and there were these people lying there sort of sodden with opium and obviously extremely poor or whatever but I suppose it was the comicalities of the situation which made it interesting for me. For instance, somebody insisted on bringing a chair for me. He produced a big wooden upright dining chair and he had to place it carefully so that the legs didn't bang on to any of these people lying on the floor and I was made to sit feeling embarrassed about it all and there was a Canadian addict there who obviously felt terribly embarrassed about it and ran off. Even that I found interesting psychologically.

Tamaya: That kind of deference accorded to Westerners—it is so awful...

Keating: For heaven's sake, it is so awful. Just in last Sunday's paper where they have a column of travellers' tales, extracts from travel books, they quoted Levi-Strauss talking about India, saying—I think rather foolishly—how subservient Indian waiters were which he found intolerable. He didn't, was not able to, accustom himself to the notion of condescending to a waiter, and he sort of bracketed it as being part of the Indian psyche, which is ridiculous of course.

Tamaya: Do you think that no parts and classes of India are the same?

Keating: Yes. I mean, I suppose statistically that it is possible you'll find 73.8 percent of Indians have certain characteristics in common.

Tamaya: I think that kind of subservience that people talk about is a fact of life there. It is depressing. But American egalitarianism takes me aback sometimes. For instance, students who sit in class with their feet up.... Does that bother you?

Keating: Yes, yes. I think when young opposed to older. Even now I tend to pat myself on the back for being able to talk to taxi drivers or whatever. I'm conscious..here I am...I mean I was brought up...I was born in 1926, pre-war, the class structure was firmly in place and I mean, my father would say to me, you are a gentleman and this was at that time...eh I was toying with the idea of writing a book about the concept of a gentleman.

Tamaya: I wish you would. My American students find it very hard to understand the English notion of gentleman—the notion of being born to a class which doesn't have to toil with their hands.

Keating: Yes, yes. It is disappearing here, everywhere...

Tamaya: To get back to the subject of subservience. What combination of factors do you think causes it, the caste system, the innate respect for authority, or colonialism?

Keating: I think colonialism just slotted into the caste system. I mean when the white Sahibs arrived, they just sort of accepted it and they did bring with them the class structure of the country. Yes.

Tamaya: It seems to me Ishiguro portrayed that in *Remains of the Day* beautifully. He shows the complex dynamics of the master-servant relationship.

Keating: I thought it was a marvelous book.

Part II

Keating: Have you heard of Elliot Gilbert? He has written a book on detective fiction that I find very useful.

Tamaya: What exactly did you find useful in Elliot Gilbert's book?

Keating: Oh...the notion that we are imprisoned in the roles we make up for ourselves. Did I give that notion to Ghote?

Tamaya: Yes. You did. Remember there is a long speech at the end of *The Body in the Billiard Room* in which Ghote waxes eloquent about how we must break out of the prison bars that we erect around ourselves.

Keating: I don't know where Gilbert got the notion...I don't think it is particularly original...but he formulates it very clearly and he uses this to say how the great detective, as Poe conceived him, was the breaker of rules in the full Romantic revolt tradition, all of which I found absolutely plausible.

Tamaya: The ultimate rule you seem to break in all your fiction is...you show how flawed logic is, how constraining logic is. Every time Ghote solves a crime, he does so by a leap of intuition.

Keating: Yes, yes. ...This is the point that Gilbert makes that a great detective is the one who is not hampered by logic. It is the solid policeman, say Lestrade, who works by logic and can't get at the ultimate answer.

Tamaya: To go back to the question of the form of the novel, Dennis Porter makes the point that the form is so conservative because the underlying assumption in detective fiction is that there is law and order, that there is logic, that ultimately things work out, that life is not irrational, that if you apply a Holmesian deductive process, all is well. That doesn't seem to be true of your fiction.

Keating: No. I mean, I am writing now in the 1990s and Porter is writing about books written in the 1950s.

Tamaya: Yes. I'm surprised that he didn't go beyond that.

Keating: This is the trouble with all of the mystery criticism really.... There is too much material.... Here I am pouring books on to you and when you think of all the parallel books which in a way if you are writing about me you should have read. Christie didn't, by any means, write the same sort of book. But it is convenient to say there is an Agatha Christie book and write about that.

Tamaya: Another point I want to bring up is...if crime is a product of the society, O.K. you say that it is the nature of society, the corruption, the injustice of society which made this crime possible. That is not true of domestic passions. For example, adultery, jealousy etc. cut across economic determinisms. To me such crimes are more interesting. It is easier to see the connection between the inadequacies of the social systems and crime. For example, Charles Manson was the child of a prostitute, was abused, and he went on to become a psychopath...that to me is predictable. What is more intriguing is when a person who has had a fairly decent life transgresses in the service of passion.

Keating: Yes, yes. Harder to write about, certainly, but much more interesting.

Tamaya: On the other hand when I talk about individual transgression, I'm talking in terms of individual psychology...which critics would say is not valid anymore.

Keating: I don't agree with it. No. I have read a certain amount of these critics. I simply don't believe it. I mean it seems to me that the individual is a fundamental thing. So there's bound to be a crime springing form the unconditioned part of us.

Tamaya: When you say that you are squarely in the tradition of the traditionalists.

Keating: That doesn't mean I'm wrong.

Tamaya: To get back to the *Sheriff of Bombay*, what I found fascinating was the way you used ordinary concrete objects, say the obscene picture which looked at one way is a perfectly ordinary picture, but you flip it and it becomes an obscene picture. It is rather like the way Shakespeare uses concrete objects, a ring or a handkerchief and it forms the underpinning of thematic concerns.

Keating: Yes. I suppose it comes from a desire for as wide a readership as possible. So that one snatches at a symbol that is ordinary. Agatha Christie with her clues which are physical objects, perfectly ordinary ones, does that.

Tamaya: They are beautifully worked into the story in a perfectly natural way.

Keating: Yes. But I have to confess, I can't remember when it occurred to me that was a symbol...

Tamaya: Did you come across a picture like that in real life?

Keating: No. I came across that and a similar device, but not an obscene one. I thought oh yes, it was obscene, then it would fit in and then I worked out how Ghote was to come across this.

Tamaya: And then that business about perception. How a person looked at one way may seem direct, honest etc, but looked at another way may seem cold, hard and ruthless. A set of virtues become a set of flaws.

Keating: I think in so far as one is tolerant. I mean tolerance is seeing the other side of things. The actual origin of that book was an absurd case that was headlines in all the papers, oh I don't know, 20 years ago, I suppose. There was this city businessman who was also an army officer or something or other who used to, used to take girls on his cruiser down the river and after a bit he would persuade them to allow him to beat them. And all this came out and it was a tremendous scandal...

Tamaya: Here in England?

Keating: Yes. Here in England. Oh...it occurred to me when he was also portrayed as being very jolly, as having romps. You know it was a truth, so to speak, you would get mostly women, who saw him as a monster of depravity and everybody was reading the story, laughing about it and there were jokes and I was very struck by it, and so it went into the back of the head and in due course it appeared.

Tamaya: He is a charming character, I thought.

Keating: Oh good. Yes, yes. I just saw him as being that person.

Tamaya: Those are some of your best books, I think: *Sheriff of Bombay, Body in the Billiard Room.* Do you agree?

Keating: Eh...I suppose I would say, *Under a Monsoon Cloud.*

Tamaya: Really?

Keating: Yes. Because...

Tamaya: I found it very hard to get through...terribly hard.

Keating: Did you? I think that's my finest book.

Tamaya: I'm really surprised. Why do you think *Under a Monsoon Cloud* your best book?

Keating: I suppose because I go deeper into Ghote than in any other. And I hope successfully...and so yes, but I'm surprised that you...I thought the court scenes, I always wanted to do a court scene and I thought that it can't help having a strong forward impetus.

Tamaya: It did, towards the end, but the whole process of disposing of the body in the rain, the first half, I found quite tedious. I had to grit my teeth and get through it.

Keating: Really...

Tamaya: I suppose you do dig much deeper into Ghote's psyche, but the whole initial premise was hard to swallow. That Ghote would actually—I mean he is a police officer—aid in concealing a body. That I find very hard to swallow.

Keating: Yes. And it is no excuse, that in fact a similar thing happened. I was told by a former commissioner in Bombay that a similar thing happened. In one of the books I have, the commissioner appears and I suddenly got cold feet that the commissioner would object and so I put in a little disclaimer and I mentioned him by name, as I happened to know him by name. And when I was in Bombay he rang me up and said that he read the book because he was mentioned in the front of it and he liked it and so would I like to meet? So very sweetly he talked to me for a couple of hours and of course, he was the investigating officer in this and they had turned the body into the sea somewhere and this very promising young inspector, I suppose he was, did commit suicide when it came out that the circumstances had been such that he accidentally killed the fellow.

Tamaya: Did you write the book after you heard his story?

Keating: Yes, yes.

Tamaya: I am beginning to wonder why I should be so surprised. After all, one reads about police corruption every day...

Keating: In America and in India it happens all the time. The reason you are shocked is because you can't see Ghote doing this...

Tamaya: It seems to me that you were liberated by travelling to India in your imagination, you were able to portray Ghote with all his hesitations, diffidence, the self-doubts. He is an endearing character because he is so human—he is not heroic, upper class, and arrogant like Sherlock Holmes. He is, however, heroic in a moral sense. He may not jump off cliffs, he is not a womanizer, he is not cast in the mold of a great detective, he is a kind of anti-hero hero.

Keating: Yes, yes.

Tamaya: It seems to me that in the creation of such a character you were further liberated because in the Western context a character like that would immediately be put down as a kind of wimp whereas in the Indian context you could make him plausible and even lovable.

Keating: Yes. I think so. If he were English I would have to have written purely comic books. Pure farce. In order to make him acceptable. You do get some detectives in some American fiction who have a little of that self-doubt.

Tamaya: P.D. James' Dalgliesh, for instance, writes poetry, he is given to introspection but he doesn't dither the way Ghote does. He is human without being comic whereas Ghote is human in a comic way and that notion of being comic fits in with the Western notion of the bumbling Indians.

Keating: Yes, yes. It does.

Tamaya: So the device worked very well for you.

Keating: Yes.

Tamaya: It was a brilliant way of writing about yourself, because you do identify with Ghote, but by making him an Indian you made the anti-heroic traits acceptable. In your early non-Ghote novels set in England, the characters never went beyond stereotypes.

Keating: Yes, yes. In those days I was writing the kind of novels Porter was complaining about.

Tamaya: You also stuck to the classic form and the novels are terribly derivative.

Keating: Yes, yes. They were derived from the Golden Age whodunits.

Tamaya: There is one character in *A Rush on the Ultimate*—Cecily Revell who is detestable—a bull dog in tweeds and pearls. She makes all these awfully racist remarks.

Keating: Yes, yes. This is an Aunt of mine who was in India. She said horrifying things about having to sit and listen to that awful music. Can you imagine saying that about magnificent music.

Tamaya: That was a satirical portrait?

Keating: Yes.

Tamaya: One of the things I ask myself when I write about you and read a lot by you is whether I'm being politically incorrect, writing about a writer so clearly in the British colonial tradition. But then I tell myself or rather, persuade myself, that you are different. For instance, in the *Sheriff of Bombay* when you talk about dancing girls, you capture the paradox of these prostitutes being very spiritual when they practice their time honored dance form. Have you seen these dancing girls yourself?

Keating: On film, yes. Ismail Merchant is a great connoisseur and in fact he was going to take me, but he was ill or something and couldn't do it and he made a little film about dancing girls—I saw the film.

Tamaya: According to Dennis Porter, Chandler's disgust for life was matched by his passion for form.

Keating: Yes. That's very English.

Tamaya: Yes. Oscar Wilde and fin de siecle. It seems to me that yours is the opposite kind of vision. In your books there is no disgust for life, rather there is much affection for the hopeless muddle that life is.

Keating: Yes, yes. I tend to see life through rose colored spectacles.

Tamaya: So it seems to me that if Chandler's disgust for life is matched by a passion for form it is "logical" that your passion is for dissecting form, spoofing form, ringing variations on the form.

Keating: That is, of course, to acknowledge form. In fact, even more strongly than Chandler really.

Tamaya: Yes. But your playing with the form implies an irreverence.

Keating: Yes, yes. One sees it as having only limited value.

Tamaya: American hard-boiled fiction is never irreverent. There is always a strain of irreverence in British fiction.

Keating: Yes, yes. That can be a fault but it has its virtues.

Tamaya: How is it a fault?

Keating: Oh, one has a suspicion that there are some things that ought to be taken seriously.

Tamaya: I thought the *Body in the Billiard Room* was full of delicious, sly literary allusions. Prof. Godbole's name, for example. Many people didn't set the allusion to E.M. Forster. Only literate readers get those in-jokes.

Keating: Yes, yes. I suppose someone like Amanda Cross overloads her novels with literary references. Although that is the reason I rather like them.

Tamaya: You do? I can't stand Kate Fansler for the same reason I can't stand Robert Parker's Susan Silverman—both are so relentlessly self-righteous about their feminism. And both seem oblivious to the fact not all woman are as privileged as they are; that there are women who are not upper class and white who have to fight for something as basic as equal wages.

Keating: Yes, yes. You know that world well. I suppose as a man I am not so irritated by that. Because it doesn't impinge on me to the same extent. I mean I don't have to think, what is my position regarding feminism. I mean, yeah. I have to think what is my position as a human being eh—looking at human beings who are women.

Tamaya: That lawyer for example, Mrs. Ahmet in *Dead on Time* seems to me is a much more admirable and real figure than Kate Fansler or Susan Silverman.

Keating: Yes, yes.

Tamaya: There she is, a Moslem, working as a public defender dealing with homelessness and yet in a curious way conforming to the strictures of her religion. And that is the way most women function. Anyway, there was a long article on current feminist criticism in *The New York Review of Books* by Helen Vendler and she pointed out Carolyn Heilbrun's (Amanda Cross) limitations.

Keating: Yes. It is comforting when you read something that agrees with what you think.

Conclusion

According to Dennis Porter,

> A critic's attitude toward a work of literature is comparable to that of a detective at the scene of a crime. A novel, like a corpse, is approached by professionals as an enigma requiring a solution. It, too, is assumed to be in need of a mediating intelligence if its true story is to be told. (226)

How does the present critic reconstruct and map out the terrain of a novelist's crime novels, if they show no signs of cessation? At the time of this writing, Keating is 65, and since he has produced, without fail, a novel a year, he may be expected to continue to do so in the ensuing years. However, since critical works, like detective fiction, are expected to have a formal conclusion, with the author's entire ouevre tidily squared away into a recognizable pattern, I will make an attempt to conclude a life and works which is far from reaching a conclusion.

Perhaps we can circle back to the beginning to Keating's ambition to be a writer. Indeed, it is well known that almost every successful mystery writer has in him/her a "regular" writer struggling to get out. (The terms "regular"/"straight" to denote fiction which is not labelled mystery, suspense etc. are

153

themselves indicative of the latter's always dubious claims to be taken seriously.) The hugely successful Conan Doyle, for example, kept spinning out Sherlock Holmes yarns while wishing he had more time for what he considered his real vocation: historical novels. In our own time the American hardboiled novelists Chandler, Macdonald and Hammett considered their mysteries indistinguishable from straight fiction and P. D. James makes no bones about casting novelistic concerns in mystery form, even as her novels become weightier and weightier.

Keating's Ghote novels fall into this murky area where detection spans not only the *disjecta membra* of crimes but philosophical conundrums as well. The ultimate riddle, of course, is the riddle of existence itself. By setting his novels in India, Keating has further complicated the issue by placing himself in the controversial territory of post-colonial fiction. Moreover, in his best work he has consistently stretched the conventions of the genre to such an extent that they barely resemble the formulaic detective novel. *The Monsoon Cloud* and *The Iciest Sin* are properly not mysteries at all, but the presence of Ghote, the sleuth, in both, ensures that they should be considered as such.

The question that needs to be asked even if we cannot expect to answer it definitively is, what place will Keating occupy in the dim future? Will he be consigned to the dustbin of literary history along with all those best-selling authors whose works the general public consumes between asleep and awake? Surely, W.H. Auden was right when he described detective fiction as an addiction (146). It is travel, beach and bedtime reading for the vast majority of people. Most consume mystery a novel at one sitting, toss it aside, begin another and neither remember the plot nor characters on the morning after.

Within the ivory towers of academia, it is a different story. The last two decades have seen a substantial change in the status of detective fiction across campuses. The proliferation of literary theories, and particularly the institutionalization of post-structuralism at places like Yale and Johns Hopkins has resulted in the serious scrutiny of popular culture because practitioners of criticism like Roland Barthes and Umberto Eco have regarded literature as one facet of cultural practice in general, and what could be more indicative of collective preoccupations than popular culture?

The more "literary" of detective fiction writers have been studied in classrooms as their works have become part of the curriculum. Robin Winks, Professor of History at Yale, regularly reviews and writes about detective fiction. When *The New York Times Book Review* published a full page review of Robert Parker's novel, and by such an eminent critic of American Literature as R.W.B. Lewis, surely there is no doubt that the humble mystery genre is in danger of getting canonized, ironically just as the canon itself is being dismantled by left-leaning theorists.

Then there is the back door to literary fame—through movies. Paul Scott, for example, wrote and published in relative obscurity till the popular PBS series *The Jewel in the Crown* catapulted him to fame and to the reissue of his books in paperback. Even Evelyn Waugh has had a posthumous rebirth after *Brideshead Revisited* was made into the enormously popular television series. Robert Parker gained even greater name recognition after the TV Spenser series. Agatha Christie continues to make money beyond the grave, thanks to films, TV series and plays. Thus, if by some lucky quirk of fate, Keating's novels were to be made into successful movies, he would achieve the kind of attention which brings in its wake respectful scrutiny. "Successful" is the operative word, however. For one of Keating's novels—*The Perfect Murder*—has been made into a movie, but alas did not achieve wide distribution.

Literary theories and fashions may come and go within ivory towers, but outside, the hoi polloi have been devoted to the lure of detective fiction. Stephen Knight and Dennis Porter, among others, have attributed the unwavering popularity of detective fiction to its formulaic, inherently conservative character. Not for mystery writers, the questioning of authority, law and order, not for them the anatomization of social ills. Responsibility falls on the individual, as does the heavy hand of justice. However, others like W.F. Stowe have dissented from this view and have argued that detective fiction should be regarded not "as mindless pastimes or anonymous cultural documents, but as self-conscious works of art" (571). According to Stowe some detective fiction writers self-consciously make the detective's traditional role as a super hero problematic and expose the problems of the social order they seek to restore. He cites as examples the work of the Sicilian novelist Leonard Sciascia whose detective's tacit collusion with evil reveals the community's "fundamental hypocrisy, its complicity with the criminals who oppress it" (576). The work of the

Swedish writers Maj Sjowall and Per Wahloo are an on-going exposé of the ills of socialist society: rampant corruption, greed, alienation, alcoholism and suicide. But Stowe rightly points out that:

> They are in no sense revolutionary: they do not incite their readers to action or expound new theories of social and economic relations. Instead, they modify a familiar literary form—the police procedural novel— to provide a memorable and at times moving embodiment of a familiar if radical critique of society. They give their readers, in other words, concrete examples of abuses and problems of which they are already aware. (577)

Keating belongs in this category. As mentioned in the introduction, Keating's Ghote novels—his best and most award winning work—take their rightful place along with the works of writers like James McClure, Van Gulik, and Tony Hillerman who use the formulaic genre to convey a highly informative but very entertaining portrait of cultures which do not dominate the world's stage and are hence not well known. McClures portrayal of the intricacies of apartheid, Van Gulik's portrayal of medieval China and Tony Hillerman's portrayal of Navajo Indians' customs and ceremonies, like Keating's portraits of India, satisfy, however minimally, every reader's wish to be blessed with the nine lives proverbially attributed to the cat. Most readers have neither the means nor the opportunity to learn about other lives, other cultures. Most of us are bound by the constraints of having to earn a living and surviving the manifold demands a job makes on our time and energy. Reading about South Africa, about Indians' burial customs, satisfies our intellectual curiosity and desire for adventure. These works confer the pleasures of travel without its risks.

Because of the arm chair travel made possible by these books, we not only observe cultural particulars but are given glimpses of how lives are lived, how human beings feel and think in different cultures. For example, elaborate purificatory ceremonies may seem irrational and superstitious when they are read about or merely observed at a distance, but when Hillerman dramatizes the men and women who practice and benefit from these rituals, they make affective sense. James McClure's graphic portrayal of apartheid, how people manage to live and relate to each other under its appalling constraints, enlarges our empathetic imagination in ways that a diligent study of laws and statistics don't. Keating's Ghote novels convey the felt lives of people under the iron grid of caste, religion and colonial history, better than mere observation or study do. The Marxist critic Raymond Williams, talking about the relationship of the individual and society in nineteenth-century fiction, says that, "Every aspect of personal life is radically affected by the quality of the general life, yet the general life is seen at its most important in completely personal terms" (200-231). This is true of Keating's best work i.e. his Ghote novels. He not only gives an accurate picture of the intricate complexity of colonialism, caste, creed and the coexistence of the past and present in India, but conveys a believable sense of how people feel and relate to each other.

There are as many reasons for the popularity of detective fiction as there are readers. Some like

Auden regard it as an addiction. Some read for the pleasures of its puzzle form, some for its social realism which as Holquist rightly points out, belongs to a post-modern esthetic with its "exterior simplicities" as opposed to the "interior complexities" with its foundations in psychology and myth, characteristic of modernism. Holquist is surely right when he points out that "the same period when the upper reaches of literature were dramatizing the limits of reason by experimenting with such irrational modes as myth and the subconscious, the lower reaches of literature were dramatizing the power of reason in such figures as Inspector Poirot and Ellery Queen" (163). Keating's detective fiction rings a further variation—while Ghote works within the conservative ideology of law and order, he relies on intuition and insists on respecting the humanity of the individual.

Keating's appeal to successive generations of readers may also lie in the curious irony of a police officer cast as an underdog—with his bumbling, his unconscious comedy, his soul-searching—which make him a far more sympathetic figure than the arrogant purveyors of reason like Holmes and Poirot. This inversion of the stereotypical sleuth of the golden-age is a strain that runs throughout Keating's fiction. Miss Unwin is that rarity, possibly an anchronistic one, of a woman sleuth in the Victorian era. Mrs. Craggs is a charwoman. The conservatism of the mystery form is sabotaged by Keating's empathy for the merely human, as opposed to the traditional, self-consciously superior sleuth. Finally it is this very subversion of British uppercrust values— the stiff-upper lip, decisiveness, sense of superiority—which save Keating from being the kind of post-colonial writer who exploits the very country which supplies him with such imaginative fodder. Keating's originality, in the end, and perhaps his passport to "immortality," is in the quiet modesty with which he overturns traditional expectations both in form and content: he is a mystery writer who plays merry havoc with the conventions of the genre, a nineteenth-century liberal humanist writing in a post-modern age, and a post-colonial writer who identifies with the colonized.

Works Cited

Bakhtin, Mikhail. *Rabaleis and His World*. Bloomington: Indiana UP, 1984.

Barthes, Roland. *S/Z*. Trans. Richard Miller. New York: Hill and Wang, 1974.

_____. *Mythologies*. Trans. Annette Lavers. New York: Hill and Wang, 1972.

Derrida, Jacques. *Of Grammatology*. Baltimore: Johns Hopkins, 1977.

Eco, Umberto. *The Name of the Rose*. New York: Harcourt Brace, 1983.

_____. *The Role of the Reader: Explorations in the Semiotics of Texts*. Bloomington: Indiana UP, 1979.

Foucault, Michel. *Discipline and Punish*. New York: Vintage Books, 1970.

_____. *The Archaeology of Knowledge*. London: Tavistock, 1972.

_____. *Power and Knowledge*: Selected Interviews and Other Writings. 1972-1977. New York: Pantheon Books, 1980.

Frazer, Sir James. *The Golden Bough: A Study in Magic and Religion*. Vol. 1. A6 Ed. New York: MacMillan, 1944.

Haycraft, Howard. "Why Do People Read Detective Stories?" *Classics and Commercials*. New York: 1946. 390-97.

Hillerman, Tony. *The Blessing Way*. New York: Harper & Row, 1970.

Holquist, Michael. "Whodunit and Other Questions: Meta-physical Detective Stories in Postwar Fiction." *New Literary History* 3 (1971-1972). Rpt. in *The Poetics of Murder: Detective Fiction and Literary Theory*. Eds. Glenn W. Most and William W. Stowe. New York: Harcourt Brace Jovanovich, 1983. 149-174

Jhabvala, Ruth. *Esmond in India*. New York: Simon and Schuster, 1990.

161

_____. *Out of India*. New York: William Morrow, 1986.

Keating, H.R.F. Personal Interview I. 4. Jan. 1983. *Clues: A Journal of Detection*, 1984.

_____. Personal Interview II. 26-27 June 1990. *Clues, A Journal of Detection*, 1992.

_____. With Maurice Keating. *Understanding Pierre Teilhard de Chardin: A Guide to The Phenomenon of Man*. London: Lutterworth P, 1969.

Knight, Stephen. *Dead Witness*, Best Australian Mysteries. New York: Penguin, 1990.

Lacan, Jacques Marie Emile. *Ecrits: A Selection*. Trans. Alan Sheridan. New York: Norton, 1977.

Macaulay, Thomas. *Speeches by Lord Macaulay with his Minute on Indian Education*. New York: AMS, 1976.

McClure, James. *The Blood of an Englishman*. New York: Harper & Row, 1980.

_____. *The Steam Pig*. New York: Harper, 1971.

Naipaul, V.S. *An Area of Darkness*. New York: Vintage Books, 1981.

_____. *India: A Wounded Civilization*. New York: Knopf, 1977.

Oates, Joyce Carol. "Adventures in Abandonment." *Review of Jean Stafford: A Biography*. By David Roberts. *New York Times Book Review* 28 Aug. 1988.

Parker, Robert. *Playmates*. Reviewed by R.W.B. Lewis. 23 Apr. 1989: 13.

Penzler, Otto, ed. *The Great Detective*. Boston: Little, Brown, 1978.

Porter, Dennis. *The Pursuit of Crime: Art and Ideology in Detective Fiction*. New Haven: Yale UP, 1981.

Said, Edward. *Orientalism*. New York: Vintage Books, 1979.

Scott, Paul. *The Raj Quartet*. New York: William Morrow, 1976.

Turner, Victor. *The Ritual Process*. Chicago: Aldine, 1969.

Van Gulik, Robert. *The Red Pavilion: A Chinese Detective Story*. New York: Scribner, 1968.

_____. *The Willow Pattern: A Chinese Detective Story*. New York: Scribner, 1965.

Williams, Raymond. "Realism and the Contemporary Novel." *Partisan Review* XXVI: 200-221.

Winks, Robin W., ed. *Detective Ficiton: A Collection of Critical Essays*. Englewood Cliffs, NJ: Prentice Hall, 1980.

Zadrozny, Mark., ed. *Contemporary Autobiography* Series. Vol. 8. Detroit: Gale Research Inc., 1988.

Primary Bibliography:
Books by H.R.F. Keating

Fiction

Death and the Visiting Firemen. London: Gollancz, 1959. New York: Doubleday, 1973.

Zen There Was Murder. London: Gollancz, 1960.

A Rush on the Ultimate. London: Gollancz, 1961. New York: Doubleday, 1982.

The Dog It Was That Died. London: Gollancz, 1962.

Death of a Fat God. London: Collins, 1963. New York: Dutton, 1966.

Is Skin-deep, Is Fatal. London: Collins, 1965. New York: Dutton, 1965.

The Strong Man. London: Heinemann, 1971.

The Underside. London: Macmillan, 1974.

A Remarkable Case of Burglary. London: Collins, 1975. New York: Doubleday, 1976.

A Long Walk to Wimbledon. London: Macmillan. 1978.

The Murder of the Maharajah. London: Collins, 1980. New York: Doubleday, 1980.

The Lucky Alphonse. London: Enigma Books, 1982.

The Governess, under pseudonym Evelyn Hervey. New York: Doubleday, 1983. London: Weidenfeld & Nicolson, 1984.

The Man of Gold, under pseudonym Evelyn Hervey. New York: Doubleday, 1985.

Mrs. Craggs: Crimes Cleaned Up. London: Buchan & Enright, 1985. New York: St. Martin's, 1985.

Into the Valley of Death, under pseudonym Evelyn Hervey. New York: Doubleday, 1986.

Inspector Ghote Series

The Perfect Murder. London: Collins, 1964. New York: Dutton, 1965.

Inspector Ghote s Good Crusade. London: Collins, 1966. New York: Dutton, 1966.

Inspector Ghote Caught in Meshes. London: Collins, 1967. New York: Dutton, 1968.

Inspector Ghote Hunts the Peacock. London: Collins, 1968. New York: Dutton, 1968.

Inspector Ghote Plays a Joker. London: Collins, 1969. New York: Dutton, 1969.

Inspector Ghote Breaks an Egg. London: Collins, 1970. New York: Doubleday, 1971.

Inspector Ghote Goes by Train. London: Collins, 1971. New York: Doubleday, 1972.

Inspector Ghote Trusts the Heart. London: Collins, 1972. New York: Doubleday, 1973.

Bats Fly Up for Inspector Ghote. London: Collins, 1974. New York: Doubleday, 1974.

Filmi, Filmi, Inspector Ghote. London: Collins, 1976. New York: Doubleday, 1977.

Inspector Ghote Draws a Line. London: Collins, 1979. New York: Doubleday, 1979.

Go West, Inspector Ghote. London: Collins, 1981. New York: Doubleday, 1984.

The Sheriff of Bombay. London: Collins, 1984. New York: Doubleday, 1984.

Under A Monsoon Cloud. London: Hutchinson, 1986. New York: Viking, 1986.

The Body in the Billiard Room. London: Hutchinson, 1987. New York: Viking, 1987.

Dead on Time. London: Hutchinson, 1988.

The Iciest Sin. New York: Mysterious P, 1990.

Nonfiction

Sherlock Holmes: The Man and His World. London: Thames & Hudson, 1979. New York: Scribner, 1979.

Murder Must Appetize. London: Lemon Tree P, 1975. New York: Mysterious P, 1981.

Great Crimes. London: St. Michael, 1982. New York: Harmony/Crown, 1982.

Writing Crime Fiction. London: A. & C. Black, 1986. New York: St. Martin's, 1987.

Crime and Mystery: The One Hundred Best Books. London: Xanadu, 1987. New York: Carroll & Graf, 1987.

Radio plays

The Dog It Was That Died. Adapted from the novel of the same title. British Broadcasting Corp., 1971.

The Affair at No. 35. British Broadcasting Corp., 1972.

Inspector Ghote and the All-bad Man. British Broadcasting Corp., 1972.

Inspector Ghote Makes a Journey. British Broadcasting Corp., 1973.

Inspector Ghote and the River Man. British Broadcasting Corp., 1974.

Editor of

Blood on My Mind: A Collection of New Pieces by Members of the Crime Writers Association about Real Crimes, Some Notable and Some Obscure. London: Macmillan, 1972.

Agatha Christie: First Lady of Crime. London: Weidenfeld & Nicolson, 1977. New York: Holt, 1977.

Crime Writers: Reflections on Crime Fiction. London: BBC Publications, 1978.

Whodunit?: A Guide to Crime, Suspense, and Spy Fiction. London: Windward, 1982. New York: Van Nostrand, 1982.

The Best of Father Brown. By G.K. Chesterton. London: Dent, 1987.

Secondary Bibliography:
Works on Keating

Clark, Meera T. "H.R.F. Keating." *Twelve Englishmen of Mystery*. Bowling Green, OH: Bowling Green State University Popular Press, 1984.

_____. "H.R. Keating: An Interview." *Clues: A Journal of Detection* 4.2 (Fall/Winter 1983).

_____. "Detective Fiction and Social Realism: H.R.F. Keating's India." *Clues: A Journal of Detection* 2.1 (Spring/Summer 1981).

Pettersson, Sven-Ingmar. "H.R.F. Keating." *Armchair Detective: A Quarterly Journal Devoted to the Appreciation of Mystery, Detective, and Suspense Fiction.* New York. 8: 277-279.

Salwak, Dale. "An Interview with H.R.F. Keating." *Clues: A Journal of Detection* 5.2 (Fall-Winter 1984): 82-96.

Sesai, Meena. "H.R.F. Keating's India and Indians: A Mystery par excellence." *The Journal of Indian Writing in English.* Karnatak, India. 9.2 (July 1981): 20-25.